Narcissistic Personality Disorder

A Complete Guide to Clearing The Confusion of NPD - Recognizing the Traits and Finding Healing After Narcissistic Abuse

Wanda Kelly

©Copyright 2022 – Wanda Kelly - All rights reserved

The content contained within this book may not be reproduced, duplicated, or transmitted without direct written permission from the author or the publisher.

Under no circumstances will any blame or legal responsibility be held against the publisher, or author, for any damages, reparation, or monetary loss due to the information contained within this book, either directly or indirectly.

Legal Notice

This book is copyright protected. This book is only for personal use. You cannot amend, distribute, sell, use, quote or paraphrase any part, or the content within this book, without the consent of the author-publisher.

Disclaimer Notice

Please note the information contained within this document is for educational and entertainment purposes only. All effort has been executed to present accurate, up to date, and reliable, complete information. No warranties of any kind are declared or implied. Readers acknowledge that the author is not engaging in the rendering of legal, financial, medical, or professional advice.

Table of Contents

Introduction... 4
Chapter 1: *History of Narcissism* 7
Chapter 2: *NPD (Narcissistic Personality Disorder)*...................... 14
Chapter 3: *Causes of Narcissistic Personality Disorder*................. 19
Chapter 4: *What Is a Narcissistic Person* 24
Chapter 5: *Different Types of Narcissists* 29
Chapter 6: *Targets of Narcissist* 37
Chapter 7: *Dealing With a Narcissist*.. 48
Chapter 8: *What is a Narcissistic Abuse?* 52
Chapter 9: *Types of Narcissistic Abuse*... 63
Chapter 10: *Divorcing a Narcissist* 66
Chapter 11: *Steps to Healing from the Narcissistic Relationship*... 73
Chapter 12: *Four Pillars for Recovery from Narcissistic Abuse* 85
Chapter 13: *The No Contact Rule* 91
Chapter 14: *Practicing Daily Affirmation*...................................... 96
Chapter 15: *Taking Back Your Life* 102
Chapter 16: *How to Avoid Another Narcissistic Relationship* 109
Conclusion 113

Introduction

Narcissistic Personality Disorder affects less than 1% of the general population. The word was originally coined by Professor Heinz Kohut in 1968. Narcissism is a prevalent pattern of grandiosity, the desire for admiration, and a lack of empathy.

There are five subtypes of Narcissistic Personality Disorder (NPD), and NPD victims may fall into one or more groups. A narcissistic personality is dishonest, treacherous, and exploitative. There are histrionic and compensatory narcissists. A fanatical form also shows signs of paranoia.

In addition, it is categorized into two forms: oblivious and hypervigilant. The indifferent person appears to be grandiose, proud, and dismissive, while the diligent person is easily hurt, oversensitive, and apologetic.

The cause of the condition is not clear, although some researchers attribute the problem to several factors such as overindulgence as a child and an over-dependence on parents. Psychotic conditions often arise early in life and wax worse over time. There are other issues due to the dependency on alcohol and drug consumption.

This book will help you in your relationship or even save someone you know who is struggling with narcissistic abuse.

A narcissist is an individual who shows extreme admiration for himself in an idealized or grandiose way mostly done to inflate the ego. A narcissist is often described as being selfish, manipulative, and demanding because they love to place a lot of attention on themselves at the expense of other people who care about them.

In the psychological world, narcissism is often viewed as a disorder called Narcissistic Personality Disorder which portrays the individual as a person lacking empathy and consideration for the emotions and well-being of others.

Friendships, relationships, family life, and every other connection the narcissist has are profoundly affected. Most disturbing is the fact that people with such behavioral traits are resistant to change even when it becomes evident that such characteristics are causing tension with others.

A narcissist often passes on the blame to others; they fail to look within themselves and see the problem as what it is. Above all, they are self-absorbed! People who have narcissistic tendencies are also extremely sensitive; they tend to react badly to criticism, disagreement, and comments because they consider them as personal attacks.

This book covers:

- The history of narcissism
- NPD (Narcissistic Personality Disorder)
- causes of Narcissistic Personality Disorder
- what is a narcissistic person

- different types of narcissists
- targets of narcissist
- dealing with a narcissist
- what is a narcissistic abuse?
- types of narcissistic abuse
- divorcing a narcissist
- steps to healing from a narcissistic relationship

And much more!

Living in reality isn't exciting for the narcissist because he already has built a fantasy world which entails a grandiose view of himself. Their idea of the world is laden by fantasies of success, brilliance, and power; and whatever opinion contradicts this delusion is either ignored or fought off entirely.

Your relationship may be significant to you, but if you are always near a narcissist, you may want to start analyzing your choices. You will discover the impact of a narcissist relationship on your mental health, but before we get there, you should know that the narcissist believes that they are better than everyone else, so how do you hold deep conversations with such a person?

To learn more about NPD, grab a copy of this book now!

Chapter 1:
History of Narcissism

The behavior we call narcissism has been around since the beginning of human history, but the term, the concept, and the disorder we call Narcissistic Personality Disorder are relatively new. Narcissism in ordinary non-scientific or psychological terms is pursuing personal gratification from egoistic vanity, essentially from admiring yourself to the extreme.

Narcissism is named after a young man in a Greek myth who fell in love with his own image in a reflecting pool. His name was Narcissus. He eventually died from grieving over a love that did not exist. In Metamorphoses, Ovid retells the tale and alludes to the story. This supposedly influenced Shakespeare's sonnets and the term self-love was used for what Narcissus was feeling.

Francis Bacon picked it up and used it in Pompey as Cicero was said to call them, "lovers of themselves without rivals." Next came Byron early in the nineteenth century, saying that self-love stings anything it stumbles upon. Finally, Baudelaire talked about self-love as being like a Narcissus of fat-headedness.

Egotism became the new word for self-love in the mid-century and lovers of self were now egotists with Freud's use of the ego and the id. Narcissism as a concept was then coined and defined within the field of psychiatry, psychology and psychoanalytic theory, by none other than Sigmund Freud.

Nacke had used the term as early as 1899, but by it, he meant a sexual pervert. Then in 1911, Otto Rank picked up where Freud left off, identifying the word as vanity and self-admiration, moving it back into the psychological realm, where it has basically stated within the Narcissistic Personality Disorder.

Still, no one has had more influence on the use of the term and the psychology of the concept than Sigmund Freud. The year was 1914 and the essay was On Narcissism, in which Freud introduced the concept and used the word. By 1968 the American Psychiatric Association included the Narcissistic Personality Disorder in its Diagnostic and Statistical Manual of Mental Disorders and associated it with megalomania.

So, for a long time, NPD and megalomania were considered to be the same thing. All megalomaniacs are narcissists, but not all narcissists are megalomaniacs.

At the same time, narcissism has been defined as a social or cultural issue, more in the line with sociological study than psychological. This is because you can be a narcissist and not have Narcissistic Personality Disorder. You will find it listed among the three dark triadic personality traits of psychopathy, narcissism, and Machiavellianism. It is also considered one of the factors in trait theory, self-report inventories like MCMI – the Million Clinical Multiaxial Inventory. From the outset, narcissism has been considered a problem for individuals and social groups. It was at the end of the nineteenth century when the term became a regular part of the language. It is used in analytic writing more than anywhere else and perhaps more than any other word.

Just like with anything else, as time goes on, the meaning of words change. This happened somewhat with narcissism too. The world today has come to mean anything on a continuum from healthy self-love to a pathological sense of self.

In the Beginning

As we said, Sigmund Freud coined the scientific term and the disorder. He discoursed it in terms of a history of megalomania and his theory that megalomania was infantile. He believed that as the person developed, they grew from egocentric to social in their orientation.

Some psychologists and psychiatrists saw megalomania as a part of the normal growth and developmental pattern of a child, while others like Kemberg saw it as pathological. The popular culture also considers megalomania and narcissism to be the same thing.

Once the concept was set loose into the culture, it blossomed. Megalomania was seen in popular terminology, novels, and movies to mean a very self-centered, uncaring individual. Just one example is the character played by Nichole Kidman in "To Die For". She wants what she wants and will do anything to get it, including murder her husband. Those who saw the film rated this character a 9 or 10 on a scale with a prototypical Narcissistic Personality Disorder person as a 10.

Others in the field did not see NPD as a separate personality disorder but as one part of the continuum of personality disorders. Alarcon and Sarabia, writing on this, claimed that NPD was not sociologically inconsistent, and more research needed to be done to consider it as a dominant trait.

Yet the concept of narcissism was central to Freud's thinking and his concept of psychotherapy. He considered narcissism to be a necessary developmental stage in growing from childhood to adulthood. In his work, he separated narcissism into Primary and Secondary Narcissism.

Primary Narcissism

Primary narcissism is the "desire and energy that drives our instinct to survive." For Freud, this included narcissism as more normal than had been thought, just a part of growing and developing. Freud claimed that narcissism complemented "the egoism of the instinct of self-preservation." What was meant by this was that we are born without an ego or a sense of ourselves as separate individuals. Then we develop the ego and primary narcissism until society intrudes with its norms and standards to insist we develop an ideal ego – or move away from primary narcissism. The ego should aspire to a perfect self, one that can move to cathect objects. Freud defined the ego libido as that which is directed only toward oneself. The object-libido is directed toward other people or objects that are outside of the self.

Secondary Narcissism

Secondary Narcissism occurs when the self moves away from those objects and people outside of itself, especially the mother. This leads the self toward the possibility of megalomania. Secondary narcissism, which is not healthy, is imposed upon primary narcissism which is healthy. Both types of narcissism develop in the normal course of human growth, but transition issues with can lead to Narcissistic Personality Disorder when you become an adult.

Freud believed the self/ego had only a certain amount of energy and if it was turned toward objects or people outside itself, then there would not be any left for narcissism. As a person develops, they move away from primary narcissism to giving their love away to others instead of keeping it for themselves.

This is healthy development, and the more love is received in return, the less likely the person is to become pathologically narcissistic. To care for someone else is to transfer the ego-libido to an object-libido by giving away one's self-love. If this love is not returned, or it is disrupted, the individual's personality balance is upset and there is the potential for a psychological upset.

Beyond Freud

Following this, Karen Horney presented a very different view of narcissism than that put forward by mainstream psychoanalytic theorists such as Kohut and Freud. Her view of narcissism did not include primary narcissism but rather, she posited that narcissism came about from the kind of early environment that poisoned the ability of the child to develop a healthy personality. Karen Horney believed that narcissism is not inherent in human nature.

Then along comes Heinz Kohut and his theory that a child is only fantasizing about having ideal parents and a grandiose self. He theorized that we all believed in the perfection in ourselves and anything we participate in. This belief in the grandiose self becomes healthy self-esteem, and the child's core values come from idealizing the parents.

Kohut believed that if the child is then traumatized, the child reverts back to the most primitive version of the narcissistic self. That version then remains primary for that person as they grow to adulthood. This becomes a Narcissistic Personality Disorder. The child does not relate to the external object but rather unites with their own idealized self-object.

He also believed that you would or could get beyond pathological narcissism either through analysis or the experiences of life. He felt if you could get beyond the pathology, you could develop ambition, ideals, and resilience for the good.

Next comes Otto Kernberg who thought narcissism was simply the role the self-played in regulating one's self-esteem. He thought infantile narcissism was normal as long as the child was exposed to the affirmation of self and "acquisition of desirable and appealing objects". These objects would then become a part of the individuals' mature and healthy self-esteem. Narcissism becomes pathological if infantile narcissism does not develop into healthy self-esteem for whatever reason.

Other important theorists since Freud include Melanie Klein, Herbert Rosenfeld, D.W. Winnicott and the French with Lacan, Bela Grumberger and Andre Green.

Narcissistic Personality Disorder Today

Today the DSM-IV contains Narcissistic Personality Disorder but there have been requests to remove it and submerge the condition into antagonism personality type domain. NPD is the "it" disorder of the twenty-first century. How will history remember our foray into this condition? There are now subtypes of narcissism that were not around before. Just to name a few, there are antisocial, prosocial, idealizing, mirroring, malignant, vulnerable, grandiose and exhibitionist.

NPD is a diagnosis that becomes more common every day. Is it just trendy or is it for some reason more prevalent? Do we truly have a

"Culture of Narcissism" as Christopher Lasch proposed in his 1979 book by the same name? He believes that NPD has become the typical way of living in American culture today.

Chapter 2:
NPD (Narcissistic Personality Disorder)

The first thing we need to take a look at is the idea of narcissism. This idea has been thrown about quite a bit, but many people are not sure what it means, how to recognize the issues that come with it, and even how to recognize when you are in a relationship with someone who has this kind of personality disorder.

Narcissistic Personality Disorder, known as one of the different types of personality disorders, is a mental condition in which people have an inflated sense of themselves and how important they are, plus a deep need to get attention and admiration from other people in high and excessive amounts. Their relationships are troubled, and they have a complete lack of empathy for anyone around them. Behind all of this loudness and a mask is a lack of confidence and a self-esteem that is fragile and vulnerable when anyone who wants to criticize them at all.

Narcissistic Personality Disorder causes problems in almost every area of life, including financial affairs, school, work, and relationships. People who have this kind of disorder are going to be pretty disappointed and unhappy when they find people who won't give them the admiration and favors that they want - the admiration that they think they deserve from everyone around them. They may find that the relationship they are in is unfulfilling and that others are not going to enjoy spending time with them because of their tendencies.

There are a few therapies for a Narcissistic Personality Disorder. The main ones include disorder centers and talk therapy. But often, the narcissist isn't even going to attempt any of this because they don't feel that they have any problems at all. They see their behavior as just fine, and their inflated sense of ego drives them to feel they deserve all of the attention that they want. And when they are not able to get it, they are justified (at least in their own minds) in acting out and using any means to get it.

There are a few different symptoms when it comes to Narcissistic Personality Disorder. The number of these symptoms and how severe they are depends on the person and the case. Some of the symptoms that come with this disorder include:

1. a sense of self-importance that is exaggerated above what it should be.
2. a sense of entitlement for the things they want. They feel like they need an excessive and constant amount of admiration from others.
3. They expect to be recognized as very superior, even though they have no achievements to warrant these feelings.
4. They take their talents and achievements and then exaggerate them.
5. They are very preoccupied with a lot of fantasies about success, beauty, the perfect mate, and their brilliance and power.
6. The narcissist believes they are superior and above others, and they only associate with people who are just as special as they perceive themselves to be.

7. They will get into a conversation and then monopolize it. At the same time, they belittle or look down on the people they think are inferior to them.
8. They think that others should provide them with special favors, and they want others to comply without any questions.
9. They are fine with taking advantage of others in order to reach the goals that they want.
10. They are unwilling or not able to recognize some of the feelings and needs of those around them.
11. They have a lot of envy for others near them, and they believe that those near them are envious of them.
12. They often have a haughty and arrogant manner. This makes them seem like they are pretentious, boastful, and conceited about getting what they want.
13. They seek admiration and getting more of what they want. They insist on having the best of everything.

Even with these things going on in the background and tainting any kind of conversation and relationship that they are trying to have with others, the narcissist is going to find that they have trouble any time they feel someone is trying to criticize something they do. This is just not something they can handle at all. When they are criticized, even if it is done to be helpful or over something very small, it is going to cause some trouble.

You will find with a narcissist that they get angry and sometimes impatient when they aren't able to get the special treatment they think they deserve. They have a lot of interpersonal problems with anyone they are near, and they feel slighted over so many trivial things. They react with contempt and outrage when things aren't going their way, and in the process, they belittle the other person in the hopes of making themselves feel better and more superior.

In addition, the narcissist runs into a lot of problems when it comes to regulating their behavior and emotions. They have violent tempers and get really upset when things are not going the way that they would like. There are times when they can't deal with the stress in their lives and adapting to any changes no matter in what area of their life it shows up is really difficult.

A narcissist is likely to feel depressed and moody because they want to reach perfection, and then they end up falling short of it. And to end this, you will find that they come with secret feelings of humiliation, vulnerability, shame, and insecurity, to name a few.

Often someone with this kind of disorder is not going to think that there is something wrong, so you won't see them going in for treatment all that often. They may do it to get the upper hand on someone else or to deal with symptoms of alcohol and drug abuse or depression. But any perceived insults to their self-esteem, such as what may happen in a therapy session, is going to be hard for the narcissist, which can make it even harder for them to accept and even follow through with their treatment.

The hardest thing for a lot of targets of narcissism to keep in mind here is that even though they may really be in love with and care about the other person in the relationship, the narcissist really has no care in the world about the target. The target is just a tool that the narcissist is allowed to use in any way they want. And when the tool or the target starts to speak up and not follow the rules, it justifies the narcissist to behave and act in any manner they want. This leaves the target feeling used and abused, and often they aren't sure how to handle this kind of situation.

It is hard to be in any kind of relationship with a narcissist, whether it is in the family, a relationship that is romantic, or even with a friend. These people are all about themselves, and they don't much care about how the other person feels in the process. They want all of the attention and love, and they want to give none of it back to others.

They can end up with some violent outbursts and other issues as well. And when all of this comes together, it is easy to see why the narcissist struggles to accept reality and deal with their different issues.

Chapter 3:
Causes of Narcissistic Personality Disorder

When looking at the statistics, the figure of approximately one percent of the population having Narcissistic Personality Disorder seems eerily high—uncomfortably high, perhaps. By now, we've built up a broad and strong idea of who is normally affected by it. As you can see, Narcissistic Personality Disorder certainly doesn't discriminate, although there are criteria that make somebody more likely to have the disorder, and it does seem to occur more commonly in men than in women.

Despite looking at the people who have Narcissistic Personality Disorder—or, rather, the groups that seem to present with this disorder the most—we still haven't looked at the huge number of root causes. The prime focus of here is looking at the different causes of Narcissistic Personality Disorder and what can actually lead to somebody to develop this horrible condition.

The exact causes of Narcissistic Personality Disorder are currently unknown. There are a number of indirect suppositions as to what causes it, and all of them culminate in the general modern vision of the development of the disorder.

The going consensus is that it is ultimately a combination of genetic, social, environmental, and biological factors. In order to dive into the big question of "why does this happen?" a bit more, we're going to look at this one-by-one in order to come to a firmer understanding of what causes Narcissistic Personality Disorder.

Firstly, let's look at the genetic aspect: there is a lot of evidence that the disorder itself can be inherited. The existence of a family member with the disorder makes it far more likely that a given individual will develop the disorder themselves. Studies performed on twins have been rather conclusive in showing an inherited aspect of the disorder.

It can be difficult, though, to determine how much of this is because of growing up with somebody who has the disorder; for example, if somebody's father were to have Narcissistic Personality Disorder. This no doubt would lead to the child taking up that influence and being, to one extent or another, impacted by the disorder. As such, Narcissistic Personality Disorder could be seen as both a genetic and a social disorder.

Beyond the genetic factors, there are a number of different environmental factors at play as well. Here, we're going to look at both the social and environmental catalysts for the development of Narcissistic Personality Disorder. These are largely thought to play the biggest part in the development of the disorder—larger than either the genetic or biological causes, with environment and biology likely playing equal parts with the environment only slightly weighted higher.

One of the largest catalysts for the development of Narcissistic Personality Disorder is when a child learns manipulative behavior from either their parents or their friends. Manipulative parents are extremely common and, unfortunately, manipulative parenting styles weren't condemned for a rather long time. With developmental psychology and emotional abuse only becoming topics largely addressed in the second half of the 20th century, the result is that there are still some rather ancient parenting styles that are incredibly unhealthy. But it doesn't just come down to one's parenting style; it also comes down to a person's general way of life. It's unfortunate, but due to the way that manipulative behavior works, it's possible for a manipulative person to surround themselves with people they can manipulate and never have to change their behavior. Because of this, they could teach or model to a child as the norm.

With attitudes on parenting largely shifting in the twenty-first century, this problem will hopefully become less and less prominent as people start to discuss things such as mental and emotional abuse more as acceptable topics of discourse. Until then, this will remain a rather prominent catalyst.

This goes hand-in-hand with another catalyst for the development of Narcissistic Personality Disorder: emotional abuse in childhood. Manipulative behavior and emotional abuse aren't necessarily one and the same, but they often go hand-in-hand. In the latter case, one may develop Narcissistic Personality Disorder as a defense or coping mechanism. Compare this to just trying to make people rationalize their position to other individuals who didn't endure emotional abuse as a child.

That isn't to say, though, that a narcissist necessarily has developed the syndrome as a defense or coping mechanism. In fact, many people develop the disorder as a result of things that happen to them in other ways. For example, a lot of people take the position that there's no such thing as excessive praise for a child. However, when a child is developing, if they stick out in any way, this will be intensely formative and cemented into their brain forever unless they make a very active attempt to unlearn it.

If somebody is excessively praised, they may develop the idea that they're unable to do any wrong. This happens often with single parents who don't wish to lose the respect or adoration of their child. Unfortunately, I've seen it pop up in quite a few cases. Likewise, if a child is excessively criticized, they may develop Narcissistic Personality Disorder as a defense mechanism.

If people tell someone all the time that they're exceptionally beautiful or talented with little basis in reality or little feedback in response to the praise, they're at risk for the development of Narcissistic Personality Disorder. If people overvalue somebody or indulge them too often, that person becomes far more likely to develop the disorder.

In essence, the mind desires some sort of equilibrium in terms of its interactions with other people. It does whatever it can to reach out for this equilibrium. Believe it or not, not all minds are equally resilient and able to this handily so they endure some of the stresses or excesses of life. In other words, a lot of what causes Narcissistic Personality Disorder can be seen as over-parenting. Someone who excessively gives praise, criticism, or manipulates their child puts their child at risk for the development of Narcissistic Personality Disorder.

Parents who are narcissists themselves will often use their children as a means of self-validation and force their narcissistic behaviors onto them. This generally leaders either to resentment or the development of the Stockholm syndrome. In the former case, people may drop all contact with their parents or limit contact as much as possible. In the latter, they often model themselves after their parents.

In terms of biological factors that correspond to the development of this disorder, there isn't a whole lot of research to work with. As said earlier, finding study opportunities for Narcissistic Personality Disorder can be difficult. However, what studies have been done have shown that the areas of the brain having to do with empathy, emotion, and compassion generally are not nearly as large as they are in neurotypical people or people without mental disorders.

One question many might ask while reading this is whether or not they can tell if their child is a narcissist. While one of the things linked to the development of Narcissistic Personality Disorder is being overly sensitive as an infant, this is only one of the signs until adolescence is reached. There are also a number of oversensitive children who don't grow up with this disorder. This means that in terms of a concrete answer, we're a little bit at a loss.

If there are other people who show signs of Narcissistic Personality Disorder, or if you tend to excessively praise your child without realistic feedback or excessively criticize them, then you may have a narcissist on your hands. However, many children and teens will show the symptoms of narcissism as a passing phase before finally growing out of it. Their brains are maturing, and they have a lot to learn about the world. Depending on how young they are, just address the manner in a reasonable way relative to their age. If you're seriously concerned or your child shows an excessive amount of the symptoms, it may not be a bad idea to set up a trip to a child psychiatrist in order to have them professionally evaluated. If they are found to have narcissism or any related psychiatric disorder, your psychiatrist will work with you and your child in order to chart a path forward.

Chapter 4:
What is a Narcissistic Person

A narcissist is a person who has a personality disorder in which he or she is excessively preoccupied with dominance, power, prestige, and vanity. They consider themselves truly superior and they need to be respected. You can call them vain or selfish; those are just some of the common labels used by many towards narcissists. They are involved in their feelings as for them it's only normal to feel hurt. They came up with this narcissist version of themselves so it can serve as the shock absorber.

There is an in grained superiority complex. This is noticeably different from confidence or healthy assertiveness. The mind of a narcissist only sees a hierarchy. To them, people are either inferior and not worth their consideration or superior and deserving of certain benefits. Of course, they perceive themselves to be in the superior bunch—if not at the very top of the pyramid. They are overcome with the need to always be right and are very likely to resort to manipulative tricks when they think they are losing an argument. This group of people make moderately good leaders, but they are extremely poor followers or team members. The narcissist believes their methods and ideas to be undebatable and would be discontent to have to follow any alternative.

Interestingly, narcissists may seek constant validation from those in their lives. Although they see everyone they interact with as beneath them, the narcissist also suffers from a fragile ego. As such, they demand approval and attention from others in both verbal and nonverbal ways. This also means that they usually cannot tolerate negative criticism, even when delivered constructively. They might go to inconsiderable lengths to maintain the narrative about their infallibility and superiority. You might be thinking that there is nothing particularly problematic about telling a narcissist that they are loved and appreciated, especially when they have done something deserving of this validation. The issue, however, is that no amount of external affirmation is ever enough. They constantly demand that their egos be caressed and are always in doubt about the way others perceive them.

This inability to be selfless and empathetic also means that narcissists are rarely ever vulnerable. This single factor, vulnerability, is responsible for longevity in relationships. Narcissists spend so much time protecting their image that they fail to emotionally connect with the people in their lives. They are, in essence, alone in their own world. Many times, narcissists are identified by how frequently they switch relationships. New romantic partnerships, for example, quickly lose their appeal, and they break-up or cheat. Although the narcissist causes pain, they are convinced that their own suffering is of more importance.

One way to offend a narcissist is by preventing events from happening in the way they imagined. And it wouldn't matter to them that you are not deliberately disrupting their plans—life happens after all. Their excruciating need to exert control over everything and everyone also causes them to be perfectionists. Working for a narcissist can be especially demanding, as these kinds of bosses may seem perpetually dissatisfied. They would complain even after their subordinates have given their best. This is because they are not as interested in the positive results as much as they want to see their personal ideas actualized in the exact way they had dreamed.

When events don't happen in accordance with the narcissist's design and there are negative results, they pass the blame to someone else. Since the narcissist considers themselves to be the epitome of perfection, they often refuse to take the blame for what is supposed to be in their charge, and they may not need a single person to assume the faults for their errors. Narcissists are not above blaming the government, their teachers, the neighborhood they grew up in, particular political parties, and so on. Usually they seek out the individual who would probably accept the blame and remain in their lives. This might be a spouse, siblings, longtime friends, or parents. Generally, these people are emotionally attached to the narcissist and can be safely blamed.

Narcissists are unlikely to show even a glimpse of weakness, but it exists. They feel shame just like everybody else. In fact, narcissists might feel it more acutely than others. They remember every time an idea was rejected, their jokes were not laughed at, or the people who could not put up with them. They begin to believe that some part of them is damaged, and they move about with insecurity. Since they chose not be vulnerable with anyone, they rarely ever find succor or healing. Their need to be seen as confident and unbreakable often supersedes their desire for peace of mind and a healthy appreciation for their strengths and weaknesses.

Narcissists are not deluded to the point of thinking that bad things cannot happen to them. They, in fact, obsess over the possibility of a mistake or mishap. Typically, they are deeply anxious individuals, which is often the result of perfectionism. However, this is also a flaw to the narcissist, and it must be hidden from public view. Some are unable to properly mask it, as their anxiety is revealed by how much they talk about all the things that could go wrong. Others are able to shove their unease to the people around them. They might point out the few times that a loved one had been negative or accuse them of being selfish. The narcissist would grow in confidence as those around them become increasingly anxious. By being manipulative in this way, the narcissist exerts their superiority.

The fact that many of us have established boundaries and respect for other people is one of the reasons friendships are maintained, the family unit still exists, and societies continue to function. Without boundaries, there would be a constant need for aggressiveness and ultimately, a lack of trust. Occasionally, we cross the line and let people take things too far with us. However, disrespecting the boundaries of others is usually the norm for narcissists. In a way, they are like babies who assume that everyone is merely an extension of themselves. They believe that the interests of other people are the same as theirs and can see nothing wrong with pushing people to achieve their own personal goals. They never expect to be rejected and might get increasingly persistent each time they are told "no".

One group of individuals bad at reading body language and other non-verbal cues are the narcissists themselves because their judgement is usually marred by personal biases. They see almost every action as a threat which must be handled with anger and defensiveness. They need people to behave dramatically to correctly interpret what their cues mean. Since they are often anxious, your words of endearment or encouragement might be misconstrued as an affront. However, they might take sarcasm seriously and assume that they are validated. If you are thinking that this might be one reason why narcissists are unable to emotionally connect with others or be empathetic, you would be right. They are either blind to subtle emotional messages or just interpret them incorrectly.

It is often a futile effort to reason with a narcissist about their manipulative and destructive behaviors. They do not understand the logic of thought processes and feelings that exist independently from theirs. They might tell you that they understand and are going to change; but, in all likelihood, this is an attempt to get you to empathize with them. As stated earlier, they believe that everyone is an extension of their perfection and everything should serve their purpose. So, they make decisions without consulting those who might be affected by them. After all, their happiness must be yours too. This logic, however twisted it may seem to you, is the only one that can be understood by a narcissist. If they are bored with a relationship, then you must be too. If they need a car that is outside the family budget, then you must be excited about it too.

Narcissists seem unable to mix the good and bad aspects of an experience, and they actively reject the holistic approach. To them, things are divided into two parts. A relationship is both good and worth enjoying or bad and must be ended. If you tried and failed to meet with the expectations of a narcissist for reasons outside your control, you might be blamed for failing, and no consideration will be given to the circumstances that hindered you. The negatives in their lives are blamed on others, while they take the credit for whatever goes right. If they cannot find someone to blame for a mistake or flaw, they bury it. The resulting shame and anxiety becomes additional fuel for more manipulative and narcissistic behaviors.

Chapter 5:
Different Types of Narcissists

Do you know your narcissistic types? Actually, there are few aside from researchers, clinicians, psychologists and psychotherapists who actually know all the types. Types really doesn't matter when you're dealing with one person. However, the type of narcissist does matter in understanding how they express themselves and how to deal with them.

Interestingly, within the three types identified by researchers, there are subtypes that typify how the typical traits may be exhibited to others.

There is some confusion among mental health professionals and researchers. Different labels are frequently used to describe the same type. Additionally, there are labels given to two unlike categories even when the same type or subtype are being described.

With all these variations of types and subtypes of narcissists, it has become difficult to grasp the type being referred to (Milstead, Ph.D., Kristen, 2018).

Three Types and Five Subtypes

Narcissism has three major types and five subtypes according to researchers. They are separately identified with different terminology by various researchers. They provide descriptions as to how they are connected to one another.

Three Types of Narcissists

1.   Classic Narcissist

Exhibitionist, Grandiose, or High-Functioning Narcissists – Most people think of these terms when they hear the word narcissist as "typical narcissists."

These are the narcissists who seek attention, expect others to flatter and praise them, brag about their achievements, and have that entitlement attitude that they should receive special treatment. This type of narcissism is the most obvious.

They see themselves as the most influential, most important person over all others. They want to make other people envious of them or elicit admiration by their boasting of their accomplishments.

This type of narcissist can be charming and have charisma. Their ambition may match the accomplishments they boast of, and you may be pulled into their admiring sphere.

If the conversation turns its focus away to anyone else, they get bored. They don't like to share the spotlight with anyone. They think they're the most important subject and rarely like sharing center stage.

It is ironic that while they're dying to be recognized and feel important, they perceive themselves as superior to the other people they meet.

2.   Malignant Narcissists

Toxic Narcissists – This is the type of narcissist that is highly exploitative and manipulative, possessing traits that are not only antisocial but are frequently compared with psychopathic and sociopathic characteristics. This type of narcissist frequently has a cruel streak that separates them from the other two major types of classical and vulnerable.

Their primary goal is to control and dominate, and to this end they will lie, cheat, steal, and use aggression and totally lack remorse for their actions. They may relish the suffering of others.

3.   Vulnerable Narcissists

Closet Narcissists, Fragile, or Compensatory – They feel superior to other people they meet but are not happy with being in the spotlight. Actually, they loathe it. They usually like to be associated with people who they feel are special rather than getting special treatment for themselves. Ingratiating others through extreme generosity or seeking sympathy to attain attention and admiration elevates their sense of self-worth (Milstead, Ph.D., Kristen, 2018).

Vulnerable narcissists can drain others emotionally. The reason is how sensitive they are in addition to how demanding. Their goal is to be seen by others as perfect creatures.

This type of narcissist is prone to becoming depressed because the fantasy life they are entitled to doesn't match the life they are living.

There are misconceptions regarding mental illness and personality disorders. Some people threaten to hurt themselves or actually do because they are looking for attention. That said, understand that vulnerable narcissists are ones that threaten to self-harm so they'll get attention. However, they rarely go through with the threat.

Vulnerable narcissists usually appear calm and introverted. However, because of the self-esteem issues they deal with, control of their emotions can still be difficult (Abby, 2018).

Five Sub-Types of Narcissists

Sub-Types 1 – Overt and Covert – Subtype 1 uses methods to get their needs met, and they are either more upfront and public or more secretive and stealthier.

Subtypes have specific characteristics. These subtypes may insult a person they perceive to be a threat because the person has a better pedigree than the narcissist. As we know, narcissists have a self-image far better than anyone else all the while protecting their fragile ego and insecurities.

Both of the Overt and Covert Subtypes will be comfortable putting a person down, be boastful, and seek opportunities to use people to fulfill their needs. However, Overt Narcissists will do so in a noticeable, public way, whereas the Covert Narcissists will be quieter and more passive-aggressive about it.

Overt Narcissists will be more out in the open about using manipulative methods to fulfil their needs. Covert narcissists will use more underhanded ways to be manipulative such that a person on the receiving end of being manipulated is not quite sure if they were manipulated or not.

A possible example of an Overt Narcissist is a Bully Narcissist. This narcissist builds themselves up by embarrassing and humiliating other people. They share traits in common with the Grandiose Narcissist. but they are cruel in the way they declare their superiority.

They frequently depend on disrespect and disdain to make others feel as if they are losers, elevating their egos and proving themselves to be winners.

They will mock and belittle the other person, and when they want something from the other person, they may become threatening if their need isn't fulfilled.

Along the line of Covert Narcissists, the Seductive Narcissist falls into this category. This type covertly manipulates the other person by making them feel good about themselves. To get the other person to do their bidding, they compliment and admire them so that, over time, the other person begins to like and admire the narcissist.

The admiration treatment will continue until the other person is no longer of use to the narcissist at which point they'll ignore them and give them the cold shoulder (Burgo Ph.D., 2015).

The Overt Subtype will always apply to the Classic Narcissist while the Covert Subtype will apply to the Vulnerable Narcissist. The Malignant Narcissist can be either the Overt or Covert subtype (Milstead, Ph.D., Kristen, 2018).

Sub-Type 2 – Somatic and Cerebral – Subtype 2 is described by what the narcissist values in themselves and others. Neither of these subtypes wishes their partner to outshine them but they do want someone around who boosts their status. Their partners are to be shown off to others as if they were objects in a collection.

Somatic narcissists are absorbed with their external appearance, how youthful they look, the clothing they buy and wear, and how well their bodies look in those clothes. They can't pass a mirror without checking out their reflection and spend an inordinate amount of time at the gym.

Cerebral narcissists think they know it all and have stellar intelligence. They're always at the ready to give their opinion even when no one asks them for it. They know more than anyone in the room about any topic, no matter what the conversation is about.

They lecture rather than have conversations and are terrible listeners because they're busy thinking about their next sentence. They try impressing others with their positions of power and achievements. All three types of narcissists can be either of these two subtypes (Milstead, Ph.D., Kristen, 2018).

Sub-Type 3 – Inverted – Subtype 3 has been found by researchers to have a specific type of vulnerable, cover narcissist known as an Inverted Narcissist. This is codependent sub-type. In order to feel special, they need to attach themselves to other narcissists. They are only happy when they have relationships with other narcissists. They suffer from abandonment issues as a child and are also called victim-narcissists.

The term so often used in arbitrary ways, making it hard to identify and taken seriously. Narcissists as a whole can be manipulative and exploitive. However, all narcissists are not alike and one type, in particular, is extremely dangerous.

Malignant Narcissists seek to dominate others and can be abusive and destructive. They lack any conscience and actually find joy in the damage they cause. Interacting with this type of narcissist can be harmful (Milstead, Ph.D., Kristen, 2018).

The Malignant Narcissist can be, by far, the most damaging. They tend to demonstrate the darker side of their self-centeredness, beyond just primarily focusing on themselves to be admired and held in extremely high regard by all who know them.

This narcissistic type wants to get their own way and doesn't care who they hurt in the process. They view the world in black and white and see others as their friends or their competition, which in their mind equals foe. They don't care about the pain they cause and they seek to win at all costs.

They may also have a sadistic streak as well as antisocial traits. Some behaviorists feel there is little difference between psychopaths and malignant narcissists.

There are other types of narcissists that fall into some of the aforementioned categories. They are not major but bear some of their characteristics.

Malignant Narcissistic Boss – This is a sad state of affairs for anyone who has this type of boss. Unfortunately, there are many in senior management and leaders whose personalities support narcissistic traits. Working under this type of narcissist can be hellish and for many, and the only way to deal with it is to get another job.

Research has shown that in leadership, there is a darker underside, and it frequently rears its ugly head when power falls into the hands of a people who develop a desire for it.

There is a culture of the "yes" staff who are frequently headed by management executives who impose their narcissism on the organization's culture.

Narcissism in the workplace is needed in some way because if an organization lacks it, there is no leadership, no path to creativity, and no self-esteem in the organization's culture.

However, narcissism that turns into a personality disorder can manifest itself in malignant narcissists at the helm who often decimate organizations and then move on to the next one. The organization had become one of "yes" regardless of how it affected the organization's culture because the Malignant Narcissist did not want to hear anything but that word. There is no check on management and no reality check (Keogh, 2017).

Vindictive Narcissist – falls under the Malignant Narcissist. This narcissist will set out to destroy another person who challenges them. If they are challenged (and the other person doesn't even realize what they've done), they will have an obsessive need to see the other declared the loser by going on a destructive rampage. The challenge can be the slightest and once provoked, this type will stop at nothing to be destructive.

They will lie about the other person, talk trash to friends and family about them, possibly aim to get them fired.

Chapter 6:
Targets of Narcissist

The victims of narcissistic abuse frequently share similar traits that mark them as easy to manipulate. While this may be unconscious on the part of the narcissist, they are attracted to a handful of traits the most conducive to the narcissist getting what he wants. When you understand what the narcissist values most in a target, you then learn how to guard yourself and not fall victim due to your own personality.

Codependent

Codependency is a sign of a dysfunctional relationship. The codependent does not acknowledge that there are any problems in the relationship. She decides to disregard or ignore her own emotions and needs because focusing on herself has never been conducive to a strong relationship or having a good time. She has learned that walking on eggshells and catering to every whim of the other person keeps the other person happy, which in turn means she is safe. She lives in denial to survive and oftentimes completely detaches herself from situations around her. She goes through the motions without really feeling anything. She walks through life and her relationship as a shell of a person, pouring every bit of herself into bettering the other person.

The narcissist loves the codependent because the codependent will always put time into pleasing the narcissist. Her own feeling of self-worth is entirely related to caring for others, to a fault. There is a good line between compassionate and codependent, and the codependent takes her kindness to the extreme of martyring herself for the narcissist's own benefit. Her intentions are kind, but the mark is missed. The narcissist is simply enabled in his behaviors, believing they are justified. This creates a destructive environment for the codependent that the narcissist thrives within.

Ultimately, the narcissist feels that the codependent is the ultimate target. The codependent already has low self-esteem, attempts to do things with good intentions, and has the intense desire to help those around her. The narcissist does not hesitate to take advantage of this, knowing that he will more easily get what he craves, and the codependent never leaves because she sees no reason to.

Caregiver Personality

Similar to the codependent, but less extreme, the caregiver personality type is quite attractive to the narcissist. While this person may not necessarily have low self-esteem, he does have good intentions and the desire to care for another individual. The caregiver naturally wants to help other people. He sees everyone as deserving of love and help and would give the shirt off his back to someone if it would better the other person's experience.

The caregiver is selfless and dedicated to bettering the lives of those around him. He is patient and willing to put up with far more abuse or mistreatment than the average person because he believes that the other person deserves to be cared for. The compassionate, patient nature of the caregiver is exactly what the narcissist needs. This person will be willing to put in the effort to ensure that the narcissist is cared for and that with some manipulation and effort on the narcissist's part, she has the potential to be browbeaten into codependency. The narcissist craves someone who is dedicated to caring for her, and the caregiver is quite likely to do so.

Empathetic

Good targets for the narcissist are empaths. Like the caregiver and codependent, those who are quite empathetic typically enjoy taking care of other people to ease their pain. The empath can feel the pain of other people so intimately it is as if she is the one being exposed to the cause of the pain herself, and she seeks to alleviate that pain in others. She does not want those around her to suffer in any way and will do whatever she can to help.

The narcissist knows this and that empaths are particularly in tune with their feelings. The narcissist can weaponize her empathy and use it against her, playing on guilt to keep her in line. He knows that the empath will be easy to manipulate simply because she is so susceptible to guilt trips. Empathy being one of her best traits becomes a weakness, and the narcissist takes advantage of it to better himself.

Has What the Narcissist Wants

This may be one of the only times the narcissist will pick out a target that is not easily manipulated or controlled. She may see someone else with what she wants and choose to befriend them to learn their secrets or have some of the benefits of their power. She will likely mirror this person quite closely, mimicking their actions to learn from them. If she is able to get close to the person who has what she wants, she may get something by default.

For example, imagine a narcissist who has befriended the mayor of a town. Any time she goes out with the mayor, she gets treated with similar levels of prestige simply because she is in the company of the mayor. Over time, knowing the mayor may even raise her own prestige in the town. If people know she is close to the mayor, they may treat her better in hopes of a good word getting back to him, and she preys on this. She can use this to her advantage and is eventually recognized in her small community, yet she has done nothing but draw the mayor into believing they are friends.

Dysfunctional or Abusive Upbringing

Those who have grown up in dysfunctional or abusive environments often never learned what healthy or normal truly looks like in regard to relationships. They never learned how to identify when something is dangerous, abnormal, or worth avoiding. All of the abuse and dysfunction became the individual's normal, which means his or her tolerance for putting up with a narcissist's abusive, manipulative antics may be far beyond what it should be.

The narcissist knows this and seeks to use it to his advantage. He knows that the one who grew up abused is not likely to understand what healthy relationships look like, and therefore, she will never understand what she is missing. She assumes whatever was modeled for her during childhood is normal and what should be expected, thinking there is nothing better beyond it.

For example, imagine you grew up with parents who hated each other's guts but could not afford to divorce while still sustaining the children. You grew up watching your parents argue and hate each other, disrespecting each other at every opportunity, and calling each other names regularly. Though you may know that your parents' relationship was not happy, you may struggle to dissociate that association with healthy relationships. You understand that they were not happy, but you are almost destined to repeat those mistakes in your own relationships and would not think twice about a partner that may behave similarly. To you, they are not as alarming and foreign as they would be to someone who grew up with parents who doted on each other. The narcissist will take that tolerance and push it to the extreme, knowing it can only benefit him and his desires.

Nonconfrontational

Those who fear or avoid confrontation simply want to live a life free of conflict. They are typically quite easygoing, and the narcissist sees this easygoing nature and desire to live without fighting and decides to take advantage of it. The narcissist's manipulation tactics require her to not be called out when she attempts to control a situation, and those who hate conflict or confrontation are the most likely to avoid calling out the narcissist's antics.

The nonconfrontational are far more likely to decide to give in to the narcissist's demands and suffer in silence than actually cause an issue, knowing that calling out the behaviors would result in exactly what the narcissist wants to avoid. It becomes a situation in which the nonconfrontational person has to decide between being miserable and not calling out the abuse or being miserable after calling out the abuse and inviting more of it.

The narcissist understands this tendency to avoid conflict and seeks out people who will not fight back. He takes advantage of the person who avoids confrontation simply because it betters his situation.

Low Self-Esteem and Lack of Confidence

Both low self-esteem and low confidence lead to someone who is easily manipulated, as both of these people crave love, but feel as though they are unworthy or undeserving of it. They feel they are impossible to love, seeing their flaws as their entire identity as opposed to just a small part of who they are. The narcissist knows this and oftentimes seeks to break down other people's self-esteem solely because those with lower self-esteem are easier to manipulate. If at all possible, the narcissist will go for someone with low self-esteem solely because she wants to get what she wants with the least amount of effort.

The path of least resistance is the path that leads to someone who already has low self-esteem or low confidence. If the person the narcissist has targeted already feels badly about himself, he will be that much easier to manipulate. The work is already half-finished, and all the narcissist has to do is add the finishing touches to groom the individual into whatever she wants.

What if I'm a Narcissist? The Narcissist's Role. At this point, you must be willing to at least try to make some changes in your behavior in to improve your own mental health and your relationship. If you are willing to do some of the work, then your relationship can be saved. But, if you still does not see any problem with your behavior, there isn't much hope for improvement. Unluckily, as much as we want to believe that we can change another person, we cannot. You can change the dynamics on your end, which can improve the relationship, but for you to actually overcome the narcissistic traits, you have to put in some effort too.

In this part, will outline some of the things you can do to improve your narcissistic tendencies. These techniques are the last step in turning a narcissist into a loving and attentive partner.

Identify the Maladaptive Behaviors That Need to be Changed

What types of behaviors do you see as maladaptive or problematic? This could come from a list that you understand to be true, or a combination of both. Once you acknowledge inappropriate behaviors, you can begin to attack and alter them head-on.

Once you know and understand the types of behaviors to work on, you can set up the positive and negative reinforcement system. Basically, if you do something positive to change a behavior, you should be rewarded somehow. It works when, for instance, you get abusive, and the people around you distance themselves to protect themselves as well as well as to cool things off.

You will eventually realize your mistake and ask to talk and deal with the problem. The punishments and rewards should be worked out, and you must be willing to commit to this. Many studies have shown that positive reinforcement works better than negative long term, so it makes sense to reward all small behaviors. If these rewards involve you, it would be a great way to strengthen your bond with others.

Practice Service to Others

People can learn to care for others. They have to choose to put the needs of another person before their own. If you are willing to try this, it will be the first step to a loving partnership. To do so, put aside one of your needs and do something no matter how simple or small whether that means running an errand you usually do, making dinner for your partner, or asking your partner to do something for her. Start with something small and over time, you will develop the ability to do more and more.

If you are willing to do these things for her, it is a good sign that you are willing to change. Talking about each other's needs and deciding what the boundaries are on both sides of the relationship is important. If you are amenable to do things for her, she should be ready to do things for you as well, especially with regard to your mental health and stability. She has the right to say no to unreasonable demands, but in a loving relationship, she have to give as well. But first, it must be reasonable.

You will learn that providing a service to others will benefit both of you, and you will develop joy from seeing your partner happy, but it takes practice.

Practice Empathy

Simply defined, empathy is the ability to put yourself in another person's place. By imagining how another person feels, you can relate to them better. The narcissist needs to be able to do this, and it is a skill that takes practice. You can understand this by asking your partner how they feel when you do a certain thing. As you begin to understand, you will put yourself in the position of another.

Don't Take Life so Seriously

To someone with narcissism, not getting their way seems like a life and death situation. But examining what happens if the narcissist doesn't get their way can make it easier to accept that horrible things will most likely not happen.

The narcissist needs to remind themselves that they are not perfect, and they do not have to be. They need to look for the humor in little things. As soon as they learn not to take life so seriously, humor can be found. And tomorrow, it probably won't even be that important.

Once you realize that even though yesterday seemed like a life and death situation, it's not the same as the present situation, and it will become easier not to take things so seriously, to laugh at your own mistakes, and to move forward in a more loving way.

When everything is no longer about you, and you face the fact that you cannot get everything you want and learn that it is not a crisis, things will get easier. You will learn to let go of these things and to move on. You do not have to have control of everything. Life will not fall apart.

Practice Self-Compassion

This is especially true if your narcissist is the grandiose type, but it is more important to practice self-compassion rather than develop self-esteem. You already have plenty of confidence, and this is what makes you think you are entitled to everything you want and desire. Instead, fostering self-compassion will also help promote tenderness in other people. And, in the end, you will change your behavior by understanding that everyone deserves love and respect. It starts with loving and respecting themselves.

To foster self-compassion, consider the three steps namely, developing self-kindness, understanding our common humanity, and practicing mindfulness.

Self-kindness is the simple idea that we should not beat ourselves up when something goes wrong. It means that when we talk to ourselves in our minds, it should be kind, rather than harsh. If you or your partner has a mistake, what thoughts go through your mind? Do you berate yourself or do you try to comfort yourself? Most narcissists will berate themselves, then lash out to make themselves feel better.

Instead of lashing out at themselves, they should practice saying kind things in their minds. Remind yourself that everyone makes mistakes and that it's okay not to be perfect because no one is. I repeat, say nice things to yourself.

Second, realizing that everyone faces the same struggles will help to connect to that common bond we call humanity. Everyone has imperfections. Everyone feels insecure at times and everyone has problems. When you practice self-compassion, you put yourself on the same level with everyone else around you. This is a necessary step for the narcissist. When they are able to do this, they can stop treating everyone else as if they are only meant to serve their needs. They will realize that they are part of a greater whole, not above it.

This will make it easier for them to change their behaviors. This is the key realization to turn a narcissist into a loving human being - that everyone comes from the same place and has issues with various roots. No one's problems or ideas are more important than another's.

Lastly, the narcissist must learn to practice mindfulness, which means keeping your thoughts in the present moment. It also means acknowledging your feelings as they happen and thus dealing with them. By suppressing what one thinks and feels, it may cause emotional outbursts later. By dealing with them in the present moment, the narcissist will be less likely to act out in negative ways.

By working through these steps, the narcissist can be turned into a thoughtful and loving person. Self-compassion, when practiced regularly, will naturally transform into compassion for the world around them. It will need much effort and will take time. Doing these things are not an easy, but the benefits for both the narcissist and you, as the partner, will be immensely gratifying.

Seek Professional Assistance

If you partner find these steps quite difficult, it can be useful to seek professional help. A therapist or counsellor can be an impartial guide as you follow these steps. They can provide the essential insight you missed and can make sure that you are not seeking to hurt other's feelings, even unintentionally. Although not necessary, a therapist can be a valuable asset in the quest of turning yourself into an unselfish, loving person.

Chapter 7:
Dealing With a Narcissist

Narcissists have a way of getting under our skin. We naturally respond by either pushing back at them or pulling away. That is exactly what they want. It is this chaos and drama that they feed off of. When you let them see what they are doing, and the damage they are causing, you are allowing them not only to hear you but to change. If they are unable to understand your pain, chances are they never will. It is sad, and it can be very difficult, but you have to take care of yourself, and sometimes this means ending the relationship.

We have selections when it comes to dealing with a narcissist.

1. Just stop trying to understand them, stop accepting their behavior, stop letting them take advantage of you, and completely cut them out of your life. Most people are going to tell you that the best way for you to deal with a narcissist is to just cut them out of your life completely. That may be true for some, but it does not have to be true for all. However, a narcissist is going to do whatever they can to ensure that every moment of your life is dedicated to serving them in some way. No one deserves to live that way.

If you always feel as if you are stuck in a relationship with a narcissist, you can end it. You should not feel any shame when it comes to ending a relationship where you have to endure the abuse of a narcissist. No one has the right to abuse you in any way, shape, or form, and you do not have to continue with the relationship.

2. Do not allow the narcissist to violate your boundaries. If they have in the past, it is time for you to build those boundaries back up and make it very clear to them that you will not allow them to violate the boundaries again.

While the best thing you could do is to remove them from your life, when it is not possible, such as when they are family, you may decide that you want to distance yourself from them. For example, if your boss is the narcissist you have to deal with, you are not capable to cut them out of your life. You could choose to switch jobs; for now, though, let's assume that you are going to stay at your job.

If your boss is the narcissist, you are going to have to isolate your work life from your home life. Even if the person is not your boss but just someone you work with, you need to guarantee that you do not let them know anything about your life outside of work. When narcissists at work start learning about our home lives, they begin collecting information that they can use against us later. Maintaining your boundaries is going to be worth it because it can save you a lot of headaches down the road.

3. Honesty is the best policy. Narcissists are pros at playing games. Because they are so good at playing these games, you may find yourself tempted to play along with their games. Do not play along! Their behavior will hurt your life or your job. If they are behaving unacceptably, make sure that you let them know. If it is possible, walk away from the situation. If the narcissist is your boss or is someone you work with, let them know that their behavior is not acceptable, then turn the focus back on to whatever it is you needed from them in the first place.

4. When you call them out and let them know that their behavior is not acceptable, you will not change what they do or the fact that they are a narcissist, but it will reduce the negativity when you do have to interact with them.

5. When you assess the situation, make sure that you are honest with yourself about what is really going on. Everyone behaves selfishly on occasion, but not everyone is selfish. When a person is a narcissist, they do not behave selfishly on occasion, but they are selfish people. Remember, the person could simply be having a terrible day, or they may have just gotten out of a terrible relationship where they were abused, and they have decided to take some time to put themselves first.

6. Refuse to engage in the narcissist's drama. Narcissists are emotional vampires. For them to feed, they have to cause drama. Never react to their behavior no matter how much it escalates. Never give any attention to their behavior. The more attention that you give to their behavior, the more it will escalate. They will do whatever they can to ensure that you are taking care of them. Once they have sucked you dry, they are going to toss you aside and search for a new victim to feed off of. They are going to do everything within their power to make you believe that everything bad that happens is completely your fault. Being blamed can cause you to lose your cool if you wear your heart on your sleeve.

When you react to a narcissist's behavior, you are communicating to them that you will tolerate their behavior. If the person has narcissistic traits and is constantly asking for your support, you need to guard yourself and make sure that you are not engaging in their drama.

7. Respond politely to the narcissist. Passive aggressiveness is not usually something recommended, but when you are dealing with a narcissist, this could be your best option. A narcissist uses name-calling and put-downs as a way to make you feel inferior to them. It increases their sense of superiority, and if they get a dramatic reaction from you, they can feed off of the negativity. When you politely respond to them, they will become bored and start looking for another victim.

Chapter 8:
What is Narcissistic Abuse?

Narcissistic abuse violence is a form of violence where the victim is exposed to narcissistic abuse trauma. One of the challenges with narcissistic abuse violence is that unlike physical violence, there might not be any physical scars as evidence. Narcissistic abuse violence happens each time the victim is subjected to emotional distress. In many cases, narcissistic abuse violence is accompanied by verbal or physical violence.

Many people are victims of narcissistic abuse violence at some point in time, but they are never aware of it. Without a proper understanding of yourself, and what your life is about, you might never know when you are under attack. It also becomes difficult to come up with effective strategies you can use to cope with the trauma from such abuse.

While anyone is susceptible to this kind of abuse, women and children are the most affected. The attacks target perceptions, feelings and thoughts. Narcissistic abuse might not be physical, but the effect on the victim's persona is just as bad.

In a relationship with a narcissistic partner, there are several symptoms, reactions and conditions that the victim might experience as a sign of abuse. The narcissist conditions the victim by creating experiences in relationships which have a negative impact. Here are some of the signs you might be suffering Narcissistic abuse in your relationship:

- Intense insecurities – your abuser identifies your personal insecurities and over time, uses them to put you down. Your insecurities grow stronger, and you cannot trust anyone.

- Disbelief in yourself – many victims' lives change for the worse because they no longer believe in themselves. Your confidence is eroded to a point where you can no longer trust your judgement.

- Incapability – victims of abuse who were once assured and competent in everything they do suddenly become incapable and uncertain about everything.

- Anxiety – you live a life of uncertainty and fear. You are constantly afraid something bad will happen. You don't trust good things because you believe the happiness is short-lived and will turn for the worst soon after. You also feel emotionally drained and incapable of enjoying true happiness.

- Indecision – victims who were once grounded become indecisive, confused and unable to trust anyone, not even themselves.

- Esteem issues – Narcissistic abuse erodes your confidence. You cannot see yourself as anything better than what your abuser says you are. You shy away from the public, afraid that everyone sees the weaknesses in you.

These are the effects of Narcissistic abuse. They manifest in different ways, but one thing is certain about them – they erode the very core of your being and your personality. If you cannot recognize yourself, how can someone else?

Narcissistic abuse violence by narcissists is meted out to victims in different categories. We will address five of the spheres of life where healthy relationships are important, and how narcissists take everything away from you.

Children and Families

- Trust issues: Life is one big frightening place for a child raised by narcissists. Strings are attached to everything, especially love. Children need unconditional love; however, children of narcissistic parents grow up learning that there is always something attached to it. Such children grow up suspicious of affection.

Interestingly enough, while such children struggle to embrace genuine affection, they are drawn to toxic relationships and affection. This happens because the feelings shared in such relationships are those that are too familiar, and they can relate. Toxic relationships become a comfortable place for such children.

It is easier for a child brought up in a narcissistic environment to trust a bad person disguised as their savior than it is for them to trust someone who is genuine and offers emotional stability.

Toxic people are an embodiment of the same challenges the children endured when growing up. Because their minds have been conditioned to embrace such instances, they are not afraid to interact with toxic people. They learn not to trust, or not to trust too much – this is easier because they have done it all their life.

- Inability to commit: Children raised in a narcissistic environment struggle with commitment issues. When you meet them, at first glance they seem like they are looking to establish commitment with someone. However, deep down they fear commitment. These kids grow up alienated by the people closest to them, so it is difficult to commit to someone or something. Commitment for such children is often on the basis of what feels right at the moment, not because they really want to commit.

Long-term relationships are not easy to get into because the feeling of being tied down to something is odd. When they encounter someone who loves them truly, it is unsettling because they have to open up about their vulnerabilities to this person, and they are not sure whether this person will stay or walk away. When you grow up alienated by family, stability and forever relationships become a fallacy to you.

Commitment to someone for such a child means that they are giving up control of their lives. Someone else is in charge of their emotions. Naturally, such children will go into defense mode to protect themselves from being hurt. They know the feeling, they have lived through it and cannot risk it again. When facing the prospect of an intense relationship, it is easier to withdraw, even without a reason. They find it easier to give up on someone who loves them and push them away, than be with them and experience unconditional love.

- Hyperactive attunement: Hyperactivity is one of the symptoms victims of abuse learn to help them cope with their abuser. It helps them know when things are about to get messy. They are keen to subtle changes in the way the abuser responds to them. This makes them realize changes in facial expression, tone and so forth. They can also identify contradiction between gestures and spoken words.

It is so exhausting to learn all this as a child. However, it is also important for them because it is the only survival technique they are aware of, which can help them avoid unnecessary pain. They grew up on the lookout for verbal, physical and emotional cues from narcissistic parents and caregivers.

This defense mechanism helps them get through a lot and protects them from the unknown. However, it also breeds a sense of prediction, which can be very unsettling for someone who is genuine but does not know how to align their words and gestures. For the child, it might be impossible to control how people react, but they can use this technique to choose the relationships they can cultivate or end.

- Afraid of intimacy: Intimacy is an emotional minefield for children raised by narcissists. When they try to open up, it is easier to share too much about their struggles in the hope that someone might feel their pain and genuinely ease their pain. The challenge here is that they often end up with toxic narcissists whose only desire is to prey on their weaknesses and exploit them for everything they have.

This is one of the reasons why such children are afraid of intimacy on in life. Intimacy requires that you open up to your partner. You have to be vulnerable around one another. You must allow your partner to see you for who you are, with all your weaknesses, embrace you and love you endlessly.

Exposure to so much hurt while growing up destroys the concept of intimacy for these children. Instead of allowing someone the chance to hurt them, it is easier to cut them off and close all avenues leading to their emotions (Yates, 2010). They crave intimacy like everyone else, but it is so huge a risk. At times, the prospect of opening up to intimacy brings back nasty memories, and it is easier to forget about intimacy altogether.

- Affinity for toxic relationships: Toxic relationships are normal for children raised by narcissists. They have a lot of experience in this, and it is easier to embrace these relationships because they almost always know what to expect. They embrace abuse as a normal thing, and that is why they find it easier to entertain people who belittle or envy them.

In early adulthood or on in life when they take stock of their friendships and relationships, they realize they have so many toxic people in their lives that they are comfortable around. This happens because they share a bond. The struggle is all too familiar, it is the only thing they know.

- Emotional sabotage: Narcissistic parents create an unhealthy relationship with their children. Children grow up afraid. They know one thing leads to another and are pessimistic about some situations. Respect and true love are foreign to them. If they come across someone who loves them unconditionally, it can be unsettling.

What does it even mean to be loved without expecting something back? How does someone even do that? This crisis sets the stage for emotional sabotage. Unconsciously, the child finds a way to sabotage that relationship because it is too good to be real. The defense mechanism for these kids is usually that anything that cannot come too close to them cannot harm them.

It is okay to protect yourself, but at times it comes at a price. Many opportunities are lost, opportunities for learning, growth, careers, and personal intimate relationships.

Relationships

A narcissist is a living example of a myth. They are no more than make-believers. They have a concept of themselves that they hope you can trust and believe. It is all lies. Narcissism has a damaging effect on relationships. Relationships require effort from both partners. As a victim, your relationship is anything but a joint effort. A narcissist partner will turn your life upside down and by the time they are done with you, you might not have the slightest idea who or what you are.

One of the difficult things in a relationship is telling whether you have a narcissistic partner or if they are overconfident. A narcissist will abuse you emotionally, leaving you feeling worthless (Lee, 2018). The following are some of the signs of emotional abuse that you need to be aware of in a relationship with a narcissist:

- Rationalizing the abuse: Abuse in a relationship hurts on so many levels. Victims of narcissists usually end up normalizing the abuse to the point where they deny it happening in the first place. You minimize and rationalize the problem. This is a survival mechanism that helps the victim dissociate from the pain of abuse. You get to a point where you feel your abuser is not a bad person. They had to react the way they did because you probably did something terrible to provoke them.

This kind of abuse happens after the victim is conditioned to believe they are helpless without the abuser. A narcissist will do all they can to ensure you rely on them for survival, and at this point, the relationship is one-sided, with the victim doing all they can to appease the abuser and meet their needs.

There are instances where the victim goes as far as shielding their narcissistic abuser from the law, instead of facing the consequences of their actions. To convince everyone but themselves that they are doing okay, some victims are conditioned as far as posting happy photos and videos of their relationship on social media, while the real story is different.

- Fear of success: Narcissists do not just take away your happiness, they take away your life. At some point, you stop doing the things you used to love. Success becomes a myth for you because it makes you happy, yet your partner hates it when you derive happiness from anything other than themselves. Talent, happiness, joy and everything else that interests you becomes a source of darkness, reprimand and reprisal.

As this continues, you become depressed, lose confidence, anxiety sets in and you learn to hide away from the spotlight, allowing your partner to shine instead. What your abuser is doing is not keeping you away from your wins because they feel you are not good enough, they do it because they are afraid your success will weaken their hold on you.

- Self-destruction and sabotage: A victim of narcissistic abuse will replay the words and actions in their minds all the time until it becomes second nature. You learn to associate certain actions in the relationship with violence and reprimand. You almost expect a negative reaction from your partner each time you do something. This amplification of negativity will grow into self-sabotage, and if your partner is a malignant narcissist, suicide might not be so far off.

Narcissists condition you to expect punishment for basically, anything. Their constant accusations, criticism and verbal abuse pushes you to a life of guilt and toxic shame, to the point where you give up on your goals, dreams, and feel worthless. You convince yourself that you are not worthy, and you don't deserve anything good.

- Unhealthy comparisons: Triangulation is one of the tactics narcissists use to manipulate their victims into submission. In a relationship, it gets worse because you end up comparing yourself to someone else all the time. When your partner keeps making you feel you are not good enough and goes as far as introducing a third party into your relationship, this is emotional terrorism. You have to fight for their approval and attention with someone else.

Comparisons are quite unhealthy. You see yourself in a different light. You wonder what they see in other people that they cannot see in you. You remember the days when your relationship was still new and wonder how you let yourself go and became worthless. It is demeaning.

- Survival through dissociation: Detachment is a survival technique that many victims of narcissistic abuse embrace. Other than detaching from their partner emotionally, they end up detaching from the environment around them. You go through life like a zombie, unable to feel anything. Your life is a mess, and you are unable to connect your emotions to physical sensations. They each exist independent of one another.

When facing a situation of emotional distress, dissociation becomes your way of life. This is the brain's way of filtering out the emotional impact of distress and pain, protecting you from having to experience the full wave of terror (Torres, Vincelette, White, & Roberts, 2013)

- Fear of the unknown: People who have experienced trauma tend to shy away from anything that might relate to it, or symptoms of the traumatic event. It might be a person, a town, a building and so forth.

As long as something reminds you of the traumatic experience, you are conditioned to avoid it altogether. The same applies to victims of narcissistic abuse.

Over time you learn to be careful about what you do and the things you say around your partner. You are happy when they are gone, but the moment they come back home, your life turns into one endless pit of darkness. Living a life where you are constantly walking on eggshells around your partner is so demoralizing.

You find yourself anxious all the time, worried that you might provoke your partner into a fit of rage. You worry about setting boundaries because your partner never seems to recognize them anyway. You want to avoid confronting your partner, and you do your best not to, but for some reason, they provoke you to get them worked up.

- Unhealthy compromises: In order to meet your narcissistic partner's needs, you have to compromise on your needs, emotional or otherwise. Everything about you comes second after your partner. Your physical safety also becomes less of a priority to your partner or yourself.

An individual who once lived a very happy and satisfying life ends up living purposely to satisfy the needs of their narcissistic partner. Many partners in such relationships give up their friendships, goals, hobbies and lives to satisfy their abusive partner. Sadly, the more you give up, the more you realize your partner will never truly be happy or satisfied with your sacrifices.

- Health problems: Many victims of narcissistic abuse develop health issues along the way. A victim who has maintained a healthy lifestyle will start gaining weight suddenly, while some will lose weight. It is also possible to develop serious health problems as a result of stress because most of the time your body works too hard to balance your cortisol levels. Your immune system also suffers from the trauma.

Sleep becomes a challenge for such people in a relationship because you don't feel safe sleeping even in your own house. You experience frequent nightmares and are dazed most of the time when you recall the trauma you have been through.

- Self-isolation: To make themselves the center of your world, narcissists will try to isolate you from everyone else in your circles. Some victims are made to quit their jobs and stay at home. The problem with this kind of isolation is that it persists to a point where the victim embraces it. The abuse you experience is shameful to you, and because you don't want people to know about it, you self-isolate.

Chapter 9:
Types of Narcissistic Abuse

Narcissistic abuse may be physical, emotional, sexual, mental or spiritual.

Verbal Abuse

Not all verbal abuse can be tagged as narcissistic. You must look at the context, frequency and the spite (hatred/vengeance) in the behavior since people often criticize, interrupt, blame, be sarcastic, oppose, block or blame you depending on what the situation may be. You must assess the frequency of this behavior. Bullying, name calling, shaming, belittling, demanding, blaming, threatening, criticizing, getting violent, accusing, undermining and ordering are all verbal abuse.

Covert Aggression

Indirectly influencing you to behave in a manner that befits the goals of the narcissist is called manipulation. You aren't verbally abused, but you are manipulated by their harmless or sweet words. Their action or words may seem to compliment you, but at a subconscious level you know you are hurt. It isn't easy to recognize this type of behavior and you often brush it off since you believe he or she loves you.

Emotional Blackmail

Emotional blackmail is common in most relationships these days. People have learnt the art of using sensitive statements or emotions to make their partner think that their partner was wrong. Emotional blackmail is another form of manipulation and may include punishment, anger, threats, intimidation or warning.

Gaslighting

Gaslighting tactics include changing the facts of events, sometimes even denying that they ever occurred. They insist that their victims imagine things and often call them crazy. The goal here is to make the victim question their own memory and sanity. The victim often feels helpless and begins to question his or her judgment, leading them to believe that they are incompetent. They become fully dependent on the narcissist. A narcissist uses this method since it is one of the best weapons in their arsenal.

Hovering

A narcissist uses this approach to rekindle the relationship with the victim if the person has chosen to leave them or has turned a deaf ear to their conversations. Often, narcissists declare their undying and unconditional love for their partners by saying they cannot move on without them. For instance, when the partner says, "I am madly in love with you. I have never felt this way before. It was only after you left I realized how much I missed you. I need you back. I am sorry. I cannot live another moment without you. Please come back," the victim gets emotional and starts to rethink his or her decision. Since love is a powerful emotion, narcissists don't fail to use it to achieve their goals.

Baiting

A narcissist baits his or her victim by pushing them over the edge to elicit an extreme emotion from them. They often taunt the victim, causing the victim to break down psychologically and emotionally.

Narcissists find this fun since they love watching their victims suffer.

Crossing the Boundaries

When someone invades your personal space, it can either lead to anger if you are mentally strong to resist or to a sense of helplessness if you are weak. Checking your mailbox, reading through your phone messages, stalking your social profiles, physically following you, denying your privacy, etc. all fall under this category.

Defaming your Character

Narcissists often spread lies about you or begin nasty rumors about you that could tarnish your reputation. This approach destroys the victim emotionally.

Physical Violence

Hitting you, throwing stuff at you, destroying your things, pulling your hair, sexually exploiting you, etc. all comes under this category.

Isolation

The narcissist will isolate you from the outside world (family, friends or social gatherings). They use verbal abuse, physical control, character assassination or emotional blackmail to achieve this.

The severity of narcissistic abuse ranges from physical to emotional; it can be violent aggression or being careless about your emotions or feelings. Although most narcissists don't feel guilty and often play the blame game, there are some capable of accepting the guilt when they begin to reflect on their actions.

Chapter 10:
Divorcing a Narcissist

Once you're sure that you want to end your marriage to a narcissist, you need to think about the next step - informing them of your decision. This can be a very difficult step to take because of the nature of a narcissist in general.

To show you the difference, consider telling someone without narcissistic traits that you want to divorce them. In most cases, you would sit down and talk about the situation, explain your side, explore the problem, and come to a mutual decision. Even if your partner wasn't in agreement completely or you didn't have the healthiest of relationships at that point, acceptance will come, and you would be able to move through the process without too much drama.

However, when you're divorcing a narcissist, things can be very different. A narcissist is likely to take the news that you want to not only leave, but divorce them, as extremely negative. They will see this as a serious slight on their character and an insult. They will twist everything around and they aim to make you change your mind and apologize for even suggesting there is a problem.

It is at this stage you need to hold tight to your reasons for wanting a divorce and not waver. If you allow yourself to move from your original decision, life will not be easy moving forward. For starters, your partner will always remind you of what you almost did, throwing it in your face as though you did something to them. If you're sure, be firm and hold tight.

Informing the narcissist that you want a divorce is something you need to think about carefully beforehand, be sure of, and then do it, almost like pulling off a Band-Aid.

This part is designed to help you choose the right time and avoid the major pitfalls that may otherwise be associated with this vital step in the route towards freeing yourself from a narcissistic marriage.

Choosing the Right Time

Choosing the right time is vital, but you should also be aware that this is not a discussion that is going to be smooth regardless of the time. You might think "what's the point in choosing a good time if it's going to go bad anyway", but that's not the right mindset to have.

Making the best of a situation is vital

Once you're sure you want a divorce, know what you're going to say. A little pre-planning will help you stay on target and ensure that you don't end up being swayed or saying the perceived "wrong" thing. You can write it down and practice it beforehand if it gives you confidence, but you need to show firmness to your narcissist.

If you show any amount of wobbling or the perception that you may not be totally sure of your choice, your partner will pounce on that and use it against you. So, think about what you're going to say and practice saying it with confidence.

Then, when you're ready, gauge the right time. Choose a time when your partner seems relatively okay, i.e., not down or stressed and not having a "moment" when they're likely to explode into a rage or a fit of passive-aggressive behavior. You might not understand your partner and their narcissism at times, but you know them best when it comes to the right time to deliver the news. Once you've identified a time which you think will work - go for it. Just do it.

If you think about it too much, you'll waver and might never end up saying it. Then, time goes on and you change your mind. If you're sure, once the time presents itself, you have to just go for it.

Do's and Don'ts

First, remember that you're giving news likely to be taken badly and also likely to cause pain. Of course, narcissists don't feel things in the same way, but you have to respect the news you're giving enough to deliver it in a way that isn't insensitive. They might throw insensitive words at you on a regular basis, but you don't have to do the same; don't bow down to their level.

The exact do's and don'ts of this type of situation really depend upon the person involved. Again, you know your partner better than we do, but there are some general ideas you can use when delivering this type of news.

Do's

- Choose your time carefully - We've just talked about this, but it's worth placing it here and reinforcing the fact that timing is everything.
- Know what you're going today and practice feeling confident with the words. If you have a close friend you can speak to, practice with them. Having someone in front of you when you say such words can be much more powerful than saying it to yourself or in the mirror. Remember, you are admitting the fact that you want to end your marriage - this is something big and something

which you can't just flippantly say in anger. It has to be done in the correct way and using the right words.

- Know that it's not going to be easy - Your partner is not just going to shrug and say "okay, I agree", they're not going to take it well. It could go a myriad of different ways, from silent treatment to rage, and everything else in-between, but you need to be aware of the fact that the discussion may be extremely difficult for you. This is where being strong and firm in your decision comes in.

- Have a plan to leave the house afterward - You don't know how your partner is going to react, and having a plan to leave the house after giving the news is a good idea. Arrange to stay with a friend or family member for a few days, perhaps until things calm down and you feel a little stronger. Being in the same space as your partner after giving this news is not going to be a happy environment, and it's likely to cause you to think back over your decision.

- Be mindful of your body language - When you're informing your partner of what you've decided, be mindful of what your body might be saying. Remember, you need to be confident and strong, even if inside you're not feeling that way at all. Hold eye contact, sit up straight, don't hold your arms across your body, and take deep breaths to control any nerves. This will help you come over as more confident and will stop the narcissist from pouncing on any perceived negative point.

- Let them know that you've taken advice - If you include a sentence that lets them know you've taken advice from a divorce lawyer, it strengthens your will and shows them you're serious.

Don'ts

- Allow yourself to be drawn into a dispute - It's very easy for a discussion such as this to turn into an argument, with accusations being thrown around. Instead, if your partner tries to make an argument, sidestep it and hold firm.
- Try and explain yourself further - It's likely that your partner is going to try and get you to give examples of the behavior you're highlighting as a problem. This is done with the lone intention to make you doubt your choices, and it's not going to be productive for you. If your partner tries to push you and get you to keep explaining yourself, remember that this is a manipulation tactic that you do not need to indulge in. Just say what you like to say and then end the conversation.
- Let your buttons be pushed - Your partner knows your sore spots and it's likely that they will try and use them at this point. Remember that to them, wanting a divorce is the biggest insult. It won't be emotionally painful to them; it will be painful for their ego. As a result, they will try and deflect that pain onto you, and they know what buttons to press. Understand this and do not let yourself react as a result of them trying to poke away at your sore spots.
- Expect anything positive - We're not negative with this point, but it's important to think of the worst-case

scenario here, and if it's a better scenario, that's good. Prepare yourself for a difficult conversation and then get out of there. If it goes well, you can pat yourself on the back and be grateful for it but expecting the worst will prepare you for anything your partner decides to throw at you.

So, what should you be prepared for?

This type of news will come over to a narcissist as the worst slight. It will hurt them, but not in the same way it would hurt you. You will feel it emotionally, and your empathy will kick in, causing you to try and see things from your partner's side. On the other hand, your partner doesn't have the empathy you do, so they're not going to see your side of the issue; they're only going to see what it does to them.

They're going to blame you for hurting their ego and self-esteem. They're going to think about how it's going to look to other people who might start to think of them in a lower way than the narcissist assumes they do now. They're going to be affronted that you dare even suggest they are anything less than the perfect husband or wife to you.

Again, expect the worst and perhaps hope for the best. It might be a negative mindset to have, but there's not a lot of positivity in this type of situation when you know that the person you're trying to explain your feelings and decision to is not going to take in the way a normally functioning human being would. Remember, narcissists do not have emotions like yours; they do not feel empathy and they do not feel the love in the same way. So, how can you expect them to take news of a pending divorce in the same way?

You can't.

In many ways, you're in uncharted territory, but focusing on yourself is the best way through it. Keep recalling what you want your future to look like and that you want to be free of feeling the way you do now. Do not let your partner sway your decisions based upon manipulation. You can see through it now and remember that it's nothing but a sadistic game to them.

Chapter 11:
Steps to Healing from a Narcissistic Relationship

Even those who understand narcissism and what it entails may struggle to deal with manipulation attempts. Though you may see the narcissist in action, if you do not understand how best to proceed in your interactions, you are still going to find yourself feeling the strains of her abuse. While the most surefire way to deal with abuse is to make it impossible to occur simply due to cutting off contact altogether, that is not always realistic or practical in real life.

Sometimes, you have no choice but to maintain some semblance of contact with the narcissist, whether it is due to having to co-parent together or you have decided that you want to wait until your children are grown before freeing yourself from the abuse. Maybe your boss is a narcissist, but you cannot afford to quit or find a new job. Regardless of the reason, there is a wide range of ways you can deal with a narcissist, from cutting them off to learning how to work with their personality flaws. However, in time, you will be able to work things out in a way that works for you. When you do learn how to deal with the narcissist's abuse tactics, however, you will likely discover the peace of mind that your life has been lacking ever since she managed to weasel her way into your life.

Acknowledge Your Abuse

Before you can begin to heal, you must first acknowledge what has happened. You must recognize that the narcissist in your life has harmed you, sometimes so much that you feel permanently ruined.

Rest assured, none of the damage is permanent if you actively try to correct it, but you must start by calling what happened what it was: abuse. You may have been taught to internalize it through long periods of being blamed and the narcissist gaslighting you into believing you are the problem, and you must learn to separate yourself from the narcissist's actions. You did not deserve the abuse; the narcissist was abusive. That is not your flaw; it is the narcissist's. You cannot control the narcissist's behavior, no matter how much you may wish you could or how much the narcissist may tell you it is your fault for provoking him. By labeling it as abuse, you begin to accept it.

Healing begins with acknowledgment. If you cannot acknowledge that what the narcissist has put you through is abuse, you may not be ready for this process. By recognizing it as the abuse it was, you will be able to take the steps necessary to correct it and heal. You will erase any of the denial you have hidden the abuse behind for however long it occurred by just naming it.

Breaking the Trauma Bond

Breaking this bond is going to be a very important when you want to get out of an abusive relationship. It is sometimes challenging, but it is possible. The first step is to decide exactly what you would like to live with and that you actually want to live in reality and not with all of the lies the abuser is sending your way. it is going to start with a denial of the illusions you have been living with, including the ones that the abuser made up for you, and any of the ones you may have made for yourself.

Remember, even if you do love that person, they are an abuser and they are not going to change. It is fine if you need to take some time to grieve this process. Many victims agree that letting go is going to feel like a real loss. You can grieve the loss of the person you thought you knew but realize that this was a façade and that person never really existed. And then be fine with letting go.

Escape in a Safe Manner

The first thing a victim needs to realize before they leave the relationship is that the narcissist is going to try to continue manipulating them. They want to bring you back to the relationship, not because they love you and need you but because they want and need the attention and adoration you sent their way.

The No Contact Rule

To make sure that you are actually able to escape from the narcissist, it is important to enforce the rule of no contact. If you feel this person is going to put you in serious danger, having a legally enforced law surrounding this order could make a difference and will ensure that you stay safe and sound the whole time.

If you do have any sort of communication with the narcissist, then you are allowing them back in and giving them the easy access that they need to manipulate you and make you stay in the relationship a bit longer. No matter what you think in the beginning, this is going to happen. If you do start to communicate with the narcissist, they are going to use all of this information against you to bring you back, and you have to start the process all over again. You have to remember that the whole abuse cycle left you weak and vulnerable, and it is much better if you can vanish and focus on your own recovery.

Cut Ties With Narcissist

When you are plagued with abuse from a narcissist, and it is practical to do so, cutting off the narcissist is the most efficient thing you can do to end the abuse. If you are not married and do not cohabitate or share children, ending a relationship is simple enough.

When you do cut off the narcissist, keep in mind that you will still be subjected to the narcissist attempts to contact you. The reason for this behavior is because he is going through an extinction burst. In psychology, an extinction burst refers to when someone who has become accustomed to a certain kind of result for a specific behavior is suddenly denied the expected result and therefore tries to get the result by desperately repeating the behavior with more and more frenzy.

Timeout From the Narcissist

Though the narcissist will be quick to accuse you of being abusive and manipulative, in true narcissistic projection fashion, you should not be swayed. Your actions are not to punish the narcissist but instead to care for yourself. You are engaging in self-care by taking a step back from a relationship that is causing you grief. That is not abusive.

Set Boundaries—and Keep Them

When contact has to be maintained, you should set boundaries. Remember, healthy boundaries are absolutely essential for healthy relationships, and while you may never have had a proper, healthy relationship with the narcissist, your boundaries will serve as barriers between you and the narcissist that will protect you from harm. These boundaries represent a clear line you draw between what is and is not acceptable. Everyone should have boundaries, including couples, as they create a baseline of expectations that you can work off to ensure that you are not stepping on anyone's toes or unintentionally angering the other person. Most people will have no issues respecting your boundaries and will do so even if they disagree with whatever the boundary you set.

The narcissist, however, does not respect boundaries. You know this as this is one of the ways they enjoy manipulating other people. When the narcissist inevitably and intentionally violates your boundaries in some way, you should quickly correct her actions. Point out that you do not agree with whatever she has done, and say that if the behavior is repeated, you will do a specific consequence. When she inevitably tests the boundary again, you MUST enforce the consequence you said would apply.

Choose Your Deal-Breakers

These are things that are absolutely not okay and warrant an immediate cut-off. These are different from boundaries in the sense that they are extreme. While your deal-breakers are essentially boundaries you have prioritized above all else, you will not give always be able to give warnings. You will never allow the narcissist to attempt to test this boundary even once before deciding to instead cut off contact the first time it happens.

These boundaries should be things you are truly passionate about not encountering. In many relationships, the most clear-cut deal-breakers are affairs, abuse, and lying. but your own may be different. If those are things that you would not tolerate in another relationship, do not tolerate it with the narcissist, no matter how much the narcissist may try to get you to give in. Your deal-breakers should remain deal-breakers no matter what.

Forgiveness and Compassion for Yourself

Forgive blaming yourself for the abuse you suffered so you can begin to celebrate the strong parts of yourself. You can forgive yourself for not leaving the relationship sooner. After all, you tried desperately to care for the narcissist, truly loving who he was, and that love was taken advantage of. Your good heart, compassion, and kindness when you see someone suffering were taken advantage of. When you recognize that, you can forgive yourself.

Remember, forgiveness does not necessarily come easy, but you deserve to forgive yourself. You did not intend for the situation to get as bad as it did, and you are making an effort to heal the best that you can. You did your best in the situation with what you had, and that is enough. Yes, you were in a bad situation for a period of time, but you survived. You were strong enough to cope as it happened and strong enough to say you are ready to get help and begin healing just by virtue of having opened this book. That deserves celebrating as you work through healing.

Grieve Properly

Grief is absolutely expected when someone dies or a relationship ends for one reason or another. We all go through grief at different periods of our lives and for different reasons. One most people do not have to go through, however, is grieving the persona the narcissist used to be when winning you over. You cared deeply for the persona that was snuffed out like a candle with no trace of it left. Likewise, if the narcissist in your life is a parent, grandparent or other family member, it is normal to grieve that relationship and that you did not get the parent or grandparent that every child deserves. Grieving is one of the steps toward healing from a loss.

Like healing from an injury, grief comes in multiple stages. Typically, five are recognized: The grieving individual will begin in denial, move on to anger, then bargaining, followed by depression and finally, he will reach acceptance for the situation. Remember, grief comes and goes in waves, and there is no true end to it. It will continue to happen throughout your life, though it grows easier to cope with as time goes by. In the beginning, it is raw and frequent, but you will find the frequency declining over time.

Release Negative Feelings

As a primary target for a narcissist, you are likely to become empathetic to some degree. As an empath, you likely have a propensity to absorb the emotions of those around you. You may have internalized some of the narcissist's own negativity because of your exposure to them. You may see some of the narcissist's negative traits in you, such as realizing that you are snapping at people the same way he snapped at you, or that you have been thinking about yourself in the way that the narcissist thought of himself. You might feel uncharacteristically angry at the world. No matter the negative feelings, you need to develop an outlet for them.

If left alone, you may feel as though your very self is festering within you, as though the toxicity from the narcissist still threatens to overwhelm you and turn you into someone you know you are not. The solution to this is to find a good outlet for yourself. Some people pour themselves into a creative hobby, such as drawing, writing, painting, music, dance, or any other form of engaging in something else. They literally channel their feelings into their art, allowing the negativity to flow through them and out into the world so it can no longer consume them. Others choose physical exercise as an outlet, choosing to sweat out the negativity with each rep of the weight set, or with each mile run. Others still may decide to nurture something else, such as growing and tending to a garden, bringing back those tender feelings that were once familiar.

Create a Support Network

As in all great endeavors, a support network is crucial. These are people you can fall back on for advice, support, or even just a quiet ear to listen in tough times. Being able to speak to other people who truly understand your struggles, your journey, and what you have gone through is incredibly validating. You feel understood and legitimized, and you will find other people who have been in your shoes who may be further down the route to healing than you are. These are people who will not try to pick apart your experiences or try to sidestep the issues you are dealing with. They understand what it means to be vulnerable to a narcissist and having them on your side will provide clearer insight for you.

Through the internet, you may also find support groups specific to the narcissistic relationship you found yourself in. With a few specific web searches, you can locate an online community for narcissistic romantic partners.

Support networks imply that you will be opening up to others about the abuse you endured in person, face to face with others. Some people are not comfortable with this idea but luckily, the internet has made finding groups of people like you easier than ever before.

Self-Care

Self-care is crucial in the period of healing. After spending so long under the narcissist's thumb and catering to him, you may find your own wellbeing quite neglected. Despite what the narcissist may have convinced you of, you deserve self-care. What better time than now to start investing in your hobbies or taking time to relax? You can take yourself on a solo date to a movie and dinner with your company or read that new book you have been dying to finish. By beginning to care for yourself, you will feel like the true you that you knew prior to the narcissist wreaking havoc in your life.

Self-care is crucial for yourself as you heal. You have spent so long catering to others, namely the narcissist, and now you deserve some pampering of your own. You deserve to go the extra mile for yourself, to treat and remind yourself that you truly appreciate the person you are, recognizing that you have one life and one body and you should appreciate what you have.

Take this time to spend some extra money on bath bombs, if that is your thing, and take a long, warm bath to soak and relax. You could get a gym membership to exercise and work on your stamina. You could decide to take a cooking class and learn to make a few new dishes for yourself now that you have the time. Anything that you have ever wanted to do goes here, so long as it is constructive and helps you feel more at ease.

When you care for yourself, make sure you are nourishing both your body and mind. Spend time every day engaging in some level of self-care, whether it is waking up an hour earlier before work to go on a walk at dawn or signing yourself up for a few classes in the evenings to finally learn those new skills. No matter what you choose, make sure you dedicate plenty of time to caring for yourself, as that level of self-care will eventually become your habitual default, and you will find yourself feeling far more well rested. By caring for yourself now, you will allow yourself to heal from the narcissist's abuse and begin to flourish as who you would have been without the narcissist's influence.

Self-Reflect

Your method of self-reflection can be anything from journaling to inner-monologues in which you explore why you were so tolerant of the abuse. Start by taking a few moments to find a quiet location and relax. You will then begin by thinking about whatever you will reflect on; perhaps your narcissist's abuse. Consider how you felt about the abuse, and write down every thought that comes to mind, a stream of consciousness style.

This lets you get everything out in the open all at once, and even if you feel the need to cry, scream, or like you do not want to keep going because it is too painful, push through anyway. The goal here is to identify everything you can about the topic, in this case, the narcissist's abusive tendencies. If you felt scared, write that down. Angry? Write that down, too. Anything is valid. After a short period of time, stop writing and put your journal away. You can return to it later.

Start Therapy

Perhaps the most obvious step, seeking therapy, is incredibly beneficial to people who have been through trauma. This can teach you how to cope with what you have been through and provide you with methods to stay strong. It also can help you identify the reasons you were seen as an easy victim to begin with and aid in remedying it. Very few people in this world do not benefit from therapy or counseling, so do not feel ashamed for needing it. There is nothing wrong with getting extra support for a serious problem and being abused would definitely classify as a traumatic or serious problem.

Trauma, especially from abuse from someone you loved and trusted, can be quite damaging to a person. You may feel as though you struggle to cope at times or that some of your insecurities that the narcissist has installed are so deeply ingrained that you will never be able to get out from underneath them. Maybe you have no clear idea of where to go with your healing and you feel like you need guidance. No matter what, whether you are coping with your abuse better or worse than average, you could benefit from seeking therapy.

Nearly every single person in this world could benefit from therapy in some form. Therapy teaches us how to better solve problems, how to cope with negativity, how to think, and sometimes just helps unpack difficult, traumatic events.

Affirmations

Affirmations have three important features: they need to be positive, about yourself, and in the present tense. So long as whatever you create meets those three standards, it has the CBT seal of approval. It is important for the affirmation to be positive because that will keep your mindset healthy and positive. It is hard to think in positives when you tell yourself, "I will never tell myself I am unworthy" as opposed to "I am worthy of the respect I demand, and I will treat myself as such." The first sentence is a negative frame of mind, and despite the fact that it has a generally positive meaning, it is still worded in such a way that you will continue to think in negatives.

By rewording it to be positive, you shift your mindset to a healthier one. The affirmation must be about yourself because ultimately, the only thing in the world you have control over is yourself. You can influence other things, but the only thing entirely within your control is you. If your affirmation focuses on someone else, you have no way to make it true, no matter how much you tell it to yourself. Lastly, keeping the affirmation in the present tense means it is currently true when you say it. Since these are said in moments of self-doubt or weakness, saying that you are currently worthy of respect or to be loved keeps you strong because you are reminding yourself it is currently true at that particular moment.

When you develop affirmations and use them regularly, you can recite them to help yourself begin shifting your own negative thoughts into ones that are far more productive.

Chapter 12:
Four Pillars for Recovery from Narcissistic Abuse

How that you have learned about the healing process and how spiritual healing works, it is time to move onto the next aspect of healing.

Just like a house that has four walls, you are also made up of four walls. These four walls or pillars are what make you the person you are and help you in creating an identity for yourself.

The four pillars are as follows:

- self-esteem
- self-worth
- self-trust
- self-love

You must have noticed that throughout the book, these words have been used generously. These are the four pillars on which every human being stands. These pillars offer the support to live life, to tackle problems that life throws at you, and to experience a fulfilled life finally.

A relationship with a narcissist hurts so much and causes internal damage because a narcissist methodically attacks all the four pillars. He guarantees that he leaves no stone unturned in damaging every small part of all the four components leaving no option for you other than to fall.

To help you understand this better, imagine a storm that is raging through. Have you ever seen the destruction a hurricane causes, and have you wondered how long it takes for the people and homes affected by the storm to reclaim their life back?

You are exactly like the person caught in a storm. A narcissist attacks you unannounced just like a storm when you least expect it or are least prepared. He attacks all your pillars and disturbs the foundation on which you are standing, so you fall and collapse just like those houses that sink in a storm or massive trees that get uprooted. The destruction is so much that it takes months and, in some cases, years for the pillars to rebuild.

Self-esteem

Self-esteem essentially means supporting yourself. It is how much control you have over yourself, your mind, your body, and your behaviors. Self-esteem is also about the perception you have about yourself and how you see yourself. The opposite of self-esteem is self-sabotage or self-damage. During the process of healing, you must build your self-confidence.

You can begin by doing simple things that tell you that you are in control of the situation. You can start by tackling basic things such as hygiene that you might be ignoring right now because of your PTSD or depression. Something as simple as having a daily routine to take a shower or dress decently even when at home can help you regain a sense of control. These baby steps will help you tackle the more significant problems.

Self-worth

This is about knowing your value and respecting your worth. It believes that you are worth the respect, love, and affection. The exact opposite of self-worth is shame and unworthiness.

After the abuse, the narcissist would have ensured that you feel a deep sense of shame and hate yourself. Self-worth is also about speaking up for your rights and standing up for yourself and what you believe in.

You need to focus on the courage to build self-worth. Courage does not mean trying to scale the mountains or running in the wild. Fearlessness means taking measures to change your life actively. It can be applying for another job, being able to negotiate good pay that you deserve, using to school if you always wanted to finish school, etc. It means identifying something that you wanted to do but have never done because you believed that you were not worth it.

Self-trust

Self-trust is about trusting yourself, your judgment. It means having faith in yourself and being confident about your decisions. It means not second-guessing every single decision and worrying about it.

When you lack self-trust, you live in constant fear and doubt. During the relationship with the narcissist, you slowly start losing self-trust without even you realize. It happens silently, and before you know it, you will be second-guessing everything. The narcissist achieves this by gaslighting and deflecting blame.

The only way to rebuild self-trust is to listen to your intuition. The gut feeling that everyone talks about is what you must pay attention to. Gut feeling is more tangible than some more forms of intuition. Gut feeling is never wrong, as it is your inner voice trying to guide you and protect you from danger or from something that is not right for you.

Your gut feeling and intuition stop working once you start ignoring them. It is like ignoring your best friend who has nothing but the best intentions for you. Once you start ignoring your intuition and gut, they no longer guide you, and that is when you take the wrong steps.

Get it back by listening to it. Follow whatever your gut says and see the change.

Self-love

Finally, the fourth pillar, self-love, is about caring and nurturing yourself. It is about treating yourself well. Self-love takes a back seat during the relationship with a narcissist because the narcissist wants and demands all the love. When you are in a relationship with a narcissist, you cease to be in a relationship with yourself. You slowly stop loving yourself and go into the self-denial and self-judgment mode. You judge yourself poorly and try to rationalize all the bad behavior being shown by the narcissist.

When you do not love yourself, you go into a people-pleasing mode and develop a savior complex. By now, you know how dangerous savior complex is to your health and sanity. You start believing you are ugly and stop taking care of your health.

The medicine to this lies in loving yourself back. This can be done by doing small steps such as cooking your favorite meal, eating healthy food, and eating regular meals. It could also be treating yourself at a salon or spa and just pampering yourself.

You can focus on the things you want to change about yourself and, more importantly, accept what you cannot change. Self-acceptance is a part of self-love because if you do not allow yourself just as you are, then there is no way that another person or the world will accept you.

This is because others will treat you just as well or as bad as you treat yourself. By treating yourself well, you are teaching the world how they must treat you and conveying your boundaries and wishes to them.

How Long Does it Take to Heal Completely?

This is a question that haunts most victims because it can seem like forever with no end in sight. A lot of days, you may go to bed wishing that you do not have to get up the next morning because you are afraid of how bad the day will be. You will always feel like there is no light at the end of the tunnel.

Do not drown in this hopelessness because this kind of negative thinking will quickly take you back to victim land. The journey to victim land is a free airplane ride where you will reach the deepest levels of fear, hatred, and disgust within minutes; but remember that journey to victim land means no return.

Countless women spend their entire lives trapped in victim land and never live a happy and fulfilled life.

The fact is that there is no timeline for healing. It is not a mathematical calculation with definite results. Do not believe anyone who tells you that it takes no more than a month or two to recover. Neither must you pay attention to your fellow victims who claim to have healed in record time. You are not in race with anyone; this is about the rest of your life, and healing needs to be thorough and deep to be sustainable.

This journey is a spiritual journey, and the destination is you. So it can be one month for some; it can take one year for some, and some people take several years. Healing depends on various factors, but above all, it depends on how committed you are to the process. At times you will see no progress at all. There will also be times when from one forward stage, you will take two steps back for reasons you cannot understand. Despite this, persist. Persistence works magic. Have a journal and write down everything so when you feel demotivated, you can turn back the pages and see how far you have come.

Celebrate each milestone and make a note of it. Acknowledgment helps develop self-love and will bring you to acceptance. Again, you need to understand that you are not in competition with anyone but yourself in this, and this not a race. Healing from narcissistic abuse is not like running a sprint, but it is more like a marathon. Hence, pace yourself and keep the momentum going.

It does not matter whether it takes a few months longer, but you must heal entirely and come out of the marathon with flying colors.

Chapter 13:
The No Contact Rule

If there is one essential rule to follow in recovering after a breakup, it is to cut off all communications with your narcissistic partner. If possible, you should also stop communicating with their friends. Maintaining contact with your ex will make it doubly hard to break free from their control.

The No-Contact Rule is a long-proven technique to help you after a breakup. Typically, you use it to make your ex miss you and get back to you. In this situation, however, you want to use the No Contact rule to detoxify yourself from your toxic ex-partners' influence. It is an incredibly effective technique, but it works better if no kids are involved.

Why is the No Contact Rule Vital in Recovering from Abusive Relationships?

After a breakup from your narcissist ex, there is one thing most people want to do. It is to go back and subject oneself to the pain and hurt all over again. It is a classic reaction after years of dependency, especially to a narcissist partner (or parent, or friend) who had complete control for years.

For the very reason that ceasing communication from a narcissistic person is critical, you are at your most vulnerable. Expect the narcissistic person to try to contact you and win you back. This is common in abusive relationships as the abuser often finds it hard to relinquish control. They cannot accept that you tried and succeeded in breaking free from their control. They do everything to be in that position again.

Narcissists by nature are predatory. Their ultimate goal is to conquer their targets to serve as their emotional sustenance. Remember that your narcissistic partner is someone who thrives on other people's undivided attention, whether positive or negative. Thus, they will do everything to make sure you, as a "source" of narcissistic supply, is there to sustain their insecure ego.

Although your narcissistic partner may likely have a long list of people as a supply, they may remain attached to you and you to them. The No Contact Rule must be in place to sever this attachment. It will be hard due to the treacherous nature of emotional abuse, but you need to stand your ground and follow the No Contact rule completely.

Your narcissistic partner will likely employ the following tactics to get you back. Familiarizing yourself with these techniques will help ensure no contact ever happens between the two of you. This is the first step in making sure you can step out of your abuser's grip and finally live a normal happy life free from emotional abuse.

Return of the Prince Charming Act

Expect your partner to remind you of the happy days you once shared. They will try to win you back with their charms, the way they did the first time you met. Expect him to do everything – even beg you to come back. There will be gifts and flowers, poems, and love letters as if you were back to courting.

But you have to remember this important fact: everything will be an act. He will only be able to sustain this for a short while. Once you've fallen for them again, they will be back to their abusive ways. Only this time, it will get worse, and they will want to punish you for trying to leave them.

The cycle of abuse happens all over again

Maintain the No Contact Rule and ignore everything they try to do. Don't reply to their messages. Never answer their calls. You may feel compelled because of your caring nature but remember that they are not a mentally healthy person. You are breaking up from someone who is extremely manipulative and cruel.

The Changed Person Act

Your narcissistic partner will tell you that they have changed to win you back. They will tell you everything they know you want to hear. They will your things will get better. It will be, that's for sure, but only for a limited time. It will be the honeymoon phase all over again. Then the abuse will come, yet again.

No one can change overnight. Real change is extremely rare for a narcissist, so you can expect that your partner will not be sincere while trying to win you back. When they are sure that they have earned back your trust, the abuse will start again, and it will get worse.

Never give in. Don't believe anything he will say or do. It will help you instead to try to learn as much as you can about their behavior. Try to determine how their mind works so you'll know the things that make him tick. It's your time to take back control.

The Sympathy Act

The narcissist will play the sympathy card just to get you back. They will try to play with your compassion. It won't come to a surprise if he dangles his own mental condition to take him back. They will try to make you feel that they need you.

They will bring up the trauma and the hardships they endured growing up, hence, their current mental state. They will make sure that you take them back by telling you that you were the only one who understood them. In turn, you will feel guilty for leaving them. So eventually you will give in.

The Manipulator

Narcissists are excellent manipulators. If they cannot get to you directly, they will try it through your loved ones. Your partner will attempt to get the sympathy of your family or friends. They will resort to being a changed person or they will use their charm.

If your family and friends don't know about the abuse or have not seen through your partner, they will most likely convince you to take your partner back.

Your narcissist partner's manipulations may not stop there. Remember that they don't want you relying on your loved ones. So, once you've gotten back with them, they will begin to ruin your relationship with your family and friends.

The Fear Factor

Fear is present throughout an abusive relationship and one of the things that keeps you bonded with a narcissist. You finally find the courage to break free, but suddenly the fear is back and so are doubt and guilt.

In most cases, victims fear three things:

1. They are afraid of losing their identity because for the longest time, the narcissistic partner defined them.

2. They are afraid of sacrificing their family, especially if there are children involved.

3. They have become financially dependent on their narcissistic partner; thus, they are afraid they won't have money to live away from their partner. The narcissist partner made sure that it will be hard to leave them.

You have to be ready when your partner uses any of the above just to win you back. When you have decided to end the relationship, be firm with your decision. And make sure the NO Contact Rule is in place.

Chapter 14:
Practicing Daily Affirmation

It is important that you undo the negative thinking habits that you developed in your relationship with a narcissist. The best way to undo these negative thinking habits is by replacing them with positive thinking. Find a way to be proud of yourself for what you have learned instead of upset with yourself for not knowing beforehand. There is nothing wrong with learning. From this experience, you have learned so much!

Think about your experience like a vaccination. Those who have yet to experience what you have are more susceptible to falling more ill than you. Getting down on yourself for having had the experience will do you no favors, nor will denying your experience.

You must understand your experience the best you can and accept your part in the matter. Once you have done that, there is no point in begrudging yourself for the part you played. The only productive next step is to move forward.

The way to move forward is with daily activities and daily affirmations that will undo your negative sense of self. The following reading is not comprehensive. It is only the start. You can find more affirmation readily available on the world wide web. The point of this part is to get you warmed up to the idea of receiving daily affirmation from yourself and acknowledging its importance to your recovery.

You Are Good Enough

Everyone is their own starting block. If you're reading this book, you like to turn to resources that help you tease out the intellectual secrets to life. You must believe that there is hope for you to feel better than you do right now. This is true.

Yet, this does not mean you are not already good enough. You are better off than a lot of people who do not believe in their own ability to improve and recover. You obviously believe in yourself and want to feel better. That means you are good enough already.

Tell yourself that you are good enough where you are to take the next step. You are always good enough where you are to take the next step. There is never a point where thinking you are too far behind will lead you to the next step.

You Deserve to be Happy

Start thinking of yourself as someone other than yourself. Think about how you would go about making yourself happy if you were someone else. Then, go about doing it. Think about what makes you happy.

It is Okay to Feel Shame Sometimes

Unlike the narcissist you were with, you know the feeling of shame pretty well. You know it because the narcissist you were with made you take on their shame. This was very generous of you. This shows that you have empathic abilities the narcissist does not possess. Yet, you took on a lot of shame that wasn't your own. This is not the appropriate way to feel shame. Your shame should be your own.

The narcissist saw you as an extension of his or herself because that's how narcissists approach the world, and they passed their shame onto you because they could not feel it in themselves. It is time for you to retrieve your shame and feel it; that's fine.

Don't overcompensate by taking up the narcissist's tricks to avoid shame. Make your shame your own. If you feel ashamed of something, ask yourself if the shame you feel is your own or someone else's. If it's your own, good! Feel it and then move on. That's all there is to it. Be proud of the truth that you can feel for yourself again, regardless of whether or not the feelings are good or bad.

Check in to see what you're feeling. Don't avoid all bad feelings. You won't recover in avoidance. Do give yourself credit for feeling your own feelings, though! This is the pathway to your recovery. Feel things but ask yourself whose feelings you're feeling.

Love Yourself for Loving Others (Even Narcissists)

Do not get down on yourself for loving someone who turned out not to be the person you thought they were. Do not get down on yourself for loving anyone. Be proud of yourself for having the capacity to love.

The appropriate response to loving someone that turned out to be bad for you is to try to find someone to love who will be good for you. Now, you have a great idea of what is bad for you. That's a very good thing. Love yourself for loving them, even if you decided in the end that it was too draining.

Enjoy the fact that you are full of so much love that you could be with a narcissist and then take steps to be with someone who can give that kind of love back to you. It is so good that you are capable of loving. You deserve to be loved back by someone else who is just as capable.

Be Proud of What You Learned from Your Experience

There is nothing helpful about thinking negatively about yourself because of this experience. You will only gain from positive thinking about your experience. Think about what you have learned. Be glad for that. Tell yourself this every time you start to think negatively about what you went through. Tell yourself that regardless of the pain caused by the narcissist, it is good that you learned enough to avoid suffering the same pain again in the future.

Be Proud of Who You Have Become

Reflect about who you were when you met the narcissist you were in a relationship with. Are you different now? How so? Instead of beating up on who you were, be proud of you are now! Think about who you have become in addition to what you have learned. Tell yourself that you are glad you have changed. Find ways to compliment yourself for being exactly who you are today.

Stop coming up with reasons to blame yourself for actions taken in the past. Start coming up with reasons to compliment yourself for the actions you are taking right now.

Be Proud of Your Boundaries

You have boundaries. They were violated for a long time. Think positively about the boundaries you set for yourself. Acknowledge them every day. Own them. The narcissist you were in a relationship probably neither respected nor understood your boundaries. This might mean you need to protect your boundaries with extra force right now. Maintain them as needed but the most important thing is that you respect yourself for having them.

You simply need to respect yourself for having them the way the narcissist did not respect you for having them. You should also understand them better than the narcissist could. Maintaining them may or may not always be a possibility. Boundaries are violated all the time. People do not always understand the boundaries of others. You cannot control these facts.

You can, however, control the way you feel about your own boundaries. The worst offense of the narcissist you were in a relationship was not violating your boundaries. They didn't know any better because they didn't understand your boundaries. The worst offense by them is that they made you feel negatively about your boundaries.

What you can control at this point is how you feel about your boundaries. You can decide which of your boundaries is worth maintaining and, in general, whether or not you feel good or bad about your boundaries. The point is to make up your own mind about the value of your boundaries. You no longer have to evaluate their merit by the standards of a narcissist who cares little for them.

Be Proud of Your Ability to Feel Shame

There has been some intentional repetition on this particular aspect of recovery because it is more difficult than affirming oneself, but the two things are not necessarily desperate. You can allow yourself to feel shame and accept the reality of your situation without thinking negatively about yourself or your situation. Once you have allowed yourself to feel shame, be proud of yourself for feeling it. Then, allow yourself to move on from it and respond appropriately.

Take the next step to feel better within the scope of reality. The narcissist you were with liked to take the easy way out of shame by imagining a new narrative. Love the narrative you know to be true even if it involves feelings like shame.

Be Proud of Your Desire to Know Reality over Fantasy

Seeking fact over fiction separates you from the narcissist you were with. You've endured the emotional abuse of their manipulation of your reality. Now, you get to choose reality and think positively about it. The narcissist you were with made you feel your fact seeking was negative (when the narcissist turned out to be wrong about something), but now you get to return to your love of reality. Be proud of the things they made you feel bad about.

Love the fact that you love the facts. Recall all of the times that they had an outburst because you simply corrected them with the facts. Appreciate the fact that you did that. It is not a bad thing that you want to know the truth. It is unfortunate that the narcissist you were with could not handle the truth when it was against them.

Be Proud of Who You Are

This is pretty close to being proud of who you have become, but as you get closer to changing your negative thinking to positive thinking, you should be thinking less about the past.

The difference between being proud of who you have become and what you learned from the experience and simply being proud of who you are in the absence of having to look back upon the relationship you had with a narcissist.

Eventually, you will want your daily affirmations to move completely away from having anything to do with the relationship you were previously in. It is important that you start by directly affirming yourself in the ways the narcissist denied you, but the next step will be affirming yourself without even thinking about the narcissist you were in a relationship with.

Chapter 15:
Taking Back Your Life

If you do choose to leave your narcissistic family, friend, or partner, there are some things you should know. It really is simple, a narcissist isn't going to shrug their shoulders and say, "Okay, see you later," and allow you to walk away. They will probably revert to their best behavior to get you back.

They do this for one reason, and that is because they hate to be rejected and take it very badly. If you leave a narcissist, you are rejecting them, and it doesn't matter how you were treated. They won't see all the manipulation and abuse they did to you. According to them, you were treated like a queen or king. They will view your walking away, and it will make them extremely angry or cut into the depths of their self-conscious. Consider if the follow happens:

- They get resentful and angry. They bombard you with posts on social media, texts, messages and calls about how they are better without you; and before they hang up, they will call you every name under the sun.
- They could be the epitome of charm again and begin reminding you of all the good times you had together.

If you realize that the first one is happening, ignore them and block them. This is just their pride taking over because they see you rejecting them. You are making a horrible mistake, and they are trying to turn the tables on you. You can see through all their scandals. Block them any way you can: their phone number, on social media, don't go to any places they frequent, and/or go stay with family or friends for a week or so if you are worried they might show up at your place. They will finally get bored and tired of no response from you.

What should you expect?

- Silence eventually
- Begging
- Insults
- Pleading
- Blame games
- Bargaining

If you think you are free and clear once the silence begins, think again. If they spot you in town soon afterward, they are going to plead and bargain with you. Getting away from them will take time, but it is a process you will be glad you started.

Dating Again

After you have gotten over the "getting rid of the narcissist" process, your future will look brighter. Most people who have gotten out of a narcissistic relationship are so traumatized by what had happened during the relationship that they don't want to get near anyone else again. When a new person begins to show the smallest inkling of something that seems like narcissism, they will run.

The truth is that everyone has signs of narcissism every now and then, but this doesn't mean we are all true narcissists. Anyone can lack empathy at times; we could belittle others without meaning to a couple of times, and we can act in horrible ways. The difference between us and a narcissist is that we apologize and see our mistakes:

a narcissist won't. Don't make a mistake of labeling everybody with the same tag.

The perfect means to get your feet back in the dating pool after getting out of the narcissistic relationship is to begin slowly. Here are some tips to help you:

- Take some time to just "be". Don't try to do things. Don't try to feel things. Don't push yourself. Take time to be by yourself and unpack the events and finally deal with them. If you need someone else's opinion or to find professional help, this is the time to do it.
- Focus on yourself. Now is the time to find things you enjoy doing and be nice to yourself. You have used up a long time with someone who was constantly unkind to you. You have probably forgotten how to pamper yourself and enjoy it. Find something you have always wanted to try.
- Think about your health. After you have focused on yourself, now pay attention to your health. Have a healthy mind and body are the best revenge ever. You really shouldn't be thinking about revenge but being a better you after you've had bad experiences will feel great. Challenge your mind, stay away from stress, get lots of sleep, indulge in some exercise, and eat healthier foods. You will soon realize how stronger you are feeling.
- Start enjoying your life again. When you begin to feel better, and it might take some time, begin to enjoy your life. Don't think about dating and don't try to meet anyone new.
- Once you are ready, be open to the possibility. The main point is to meet somebody worthy of your attention and time,

somebody who will give you what you didn't have before. You don't need anyone who can heal or complete you. If you think you are ready, just be open to meeting people but don't put any importance on it. People who have gotten out of narcissistic relationship might be needy since they are desperately trying not to let it happen again. If you can follow these steps and put importance on building yourself back up, this shouldn't happen to you.

- Don't think that everybody is going to act like your ex. If you do find somebody and decide to begin dating, don't put them in the same boat as your ex. This is extremely important. True narcissists are extremely rare, and you need to remember this. It is very unlikely that you will meet someone who is a narcissist twice in one lifetime. Yes, it might be possible that you will meet somebody who will act a tad bit narcissistic occasionally, but they aren't a true narcissist and won't bring the same problems to the relationship.
- Recognize the signs. If anyone begins to treat you horribly, address the problem and stand firm before you walk away. If living through a narcissist relationship teaches you anything, it will be that you aren't going to let the same thing happen again.

If you are thinking that you won't ever try to date again, saying I am fine being by myself, it is time to ask yourself why you are feeling this way. Do you really not want a relationship and want to be alone? You want to travel or reconnect with friends you let slip away. Are you just saying it because you are scared of being hurt again?

Some people really don't want another relationship, and this is perfectly fine if is for the correct reasons. If you are just staying away from romantic connections because you are afraid, this is something you need to address early on. You might find your feelings will change with time but don't remain closed off to connections just because your past was cloudy. This judgment is going to hurt you more in the long run.

You must remember that you deserve to be loved, and it doesn't matter what you were forced to believe in the past.

What happens to a narcissist who won't get help?

We have covered a lot of information about the victim's future but what about the narcissist's future. It isn't a nice picture if the narcissist won't get help. If they don't, they will likely jump from one relationship to the next. If they do find a long-term relationship, their partner won't be fulfilled and happy. They will more than likely just be putting up with the narcissist.

If during the duration of the narcissist's relationship, the couple has children, the bad news is the children will probably develop narcissist behaviors since they will be exposed to it through their growing years. Even though there isn't a definite answer to what causes narcissism, there are suggestions that experiences during childhood have firm links to developing the disorder during their adolescent or adult years.

Narcissists are known to become bitter with time. This is mainly due to people coming into their lives and then leaving , and they can't figure out why. They will always put the blame onto someone else and will never see the role they had in the person leaving. Most narcissistic traits get worse with age as they experience more things through their life.

You can see it is a very bleak picture; this is the sad truth about the narcissist's life. People will only stay around if they are treated nicely. If they get treated like crap, they will eventually leave. Some might not get to that point, but relationships with narcissists are usually empty and don't have respect and true love.

The biggest price any narcissist will pay for their actions over time will be loneliness and not ever knowing what a meaningful relationship really is. The deepest and most meaningful relationship a narcissist will have will be with themselves.

Should we blame social elements?

You almost know all there is to know about narcissists and the issues and traits that go with it. We also need to look at another area. Are social elements to blame for the increasing number of narcissists?

True narcissists are very rare, but it is a term that we hear more and more. For this reason, narcissistic behaviors are more common now, so we need to find out why. Is it all the social pressures we have to deal with? Is it social media? Is it because we are pressured to own the best, look the best, and be the best?

Social media makes us aware of the way other people live and look. The influences of social media tell us that if we want to be the best, we must look our best, often meaning we have to use a certain product. We get bombarded with selfies and full body photos that us filters and Photoshop to change their appearance drastically. The majority of what we see just isn't real. Now do you wonder why we have all these unrealistic expectations of what we should look like, what we should be, and what we need to aim for?

No one is completely sure what causes narcissism, but it is the things we are exposed to in life. Most narcissistic cases are thought to come from things we experienced during childhood, but what caused those experiences? What makes someone act in a specific way? What makes someone create trauma for another human that then causes them to develop a certain personality disorder? It is hard to figure out, but you have to take into account all the possibilities.

Chapter 16:
How to Avoid Another Narcissistic Relationship

How can you recognize a narcissist from the first date? If you are ignorant of who a narcissist is and how to spot them quickly, you will most likely fall into their trap. This part will enlighten you on how to recognize a narcissist from the first date. I won't feed you lies; identifying a narcissistic individual may be complicated. It takes lots of focus and concentration to spot the difference because they are highly skilled manipulators.

How does the narcissist appears on the first date?

Narcissists are very confident people. Once they spot their prey, they make a move and will do anything in their power to get that person. They are really persuasive people. On your first date with a narcissist, he will appear very charming and "too good" for you. Don't get me wrong, an average guy that really likes you can look this way too. But there's something out of the ordinary when it comes to a narcissist. He could get a Lamborghini just to impress you. Just about anything to hook you. If you notice any "too good to be true" kind of signs on your first date, that's a red flag.

Narcissists like to be in control of anything around them. They believe they are the best at everything. Let's say he planned dinner for two at a restaurant and you thought it was just something casual.

What they say

Another easy way to spot a narcissist on a first date is in what they say. From the way a person talks on the first date, you can deduce whether he's a narcissist or not. You just have to pay close attention. Narcissists are attention lovers; they'll do anything to keep the attention focused on them. They like everyone to know how successful they are. If on your first date, your date can't seem to stop talking about himself, that's a massive red flag. A narcissist will always try to direct all the attention to himself. They try to make each topic of discussion about them. If you notice this kind of attitude on your first date, there's no need for a second date.

Narcissists are good lovers on the first date. They can say, "Do you believe in love at first sight?" Don't fall that easily! Wait for some other good signs before you jump into the wagon. Often times, toxic relationships are delightful in the beginning, especially on the first date. It could appear to be your best date since you've been dating. They could also say something like, "We have so much in common." Narcissists are cunning and manipulative. They ask a lot of questions on the first date just to know a lot about you. They want to know all about you but say little about themselves. Be careful! Do not reveal everything to them.

Lastly, narcissists always have a history of crazy exes. They may say, "My ex dumped me and left me heartbroken" or "My last few relationships have been awful." That's the durable quality of a narcissist. Narcissists are far from accountable or responsible for anything. When you notice that he keeps talking about what they did to him in his last relationships without having any fault whatsoever, that's a red flag.

The signs your date is a narcissist

The Conversation

When on a date with someone, the primary purpose is to get to know each other, right? This is quite different from a narcissist. When on a date with a narcissist, the conversation becomes a monologue instead of a dialogue. He does all the talking, leaving little or no room for the other party to talk. They brag about themselves, their business, how they landed their first million, and so on.

Distraction

We said earlier that narcissists love attention, right? Each time you get distracted by something, they get really annoyed with you. They never want focus shifted away from them. They want to be the center of discussion; they want to be in control. Stay alert!

Special Treatment

Narcissists are so full of themselves. They have this belief that they should be treated specially. They plan your first date without acknowledging your opinion at all. On the first date, they may demand to change their sitting arrangements or quarrel with the waiter for something not worth it.

Impatient

Narcissists are very anxious individuals. They've no patience whatsoever. On your first date with a narcissist, he will most likely cause a scene with the manager of the restaurant he picked himself.

Critiques

One last thing you have to look out for on your date is that narcissists are nasty critics. They are not satisfied with anything. They believe no one is better than them and what they are doing is the best.

How can you avoid the rest of the date?

After you've concluded that your date is a narcissist, you are halfway safe. What's remaining is how to avoid the remaining part of the date. Firstly, avoid feeding his ego by complimenting him on what he did or how he looks. Ask him a lot of questions and ensure he answers them. Make him feel intimidated and less in control. You can brag too, appear influential, and highly esteemed. Try to disagree with whatever he says to you.

Maybe he tells you very sweet and charming things, so say something to counteract it. For instance, if he says something like, '"he first time I set my eyes on you…" try to say something mean that will make him feel you don't care. Deep down, narcissists are sad and have low self-esteem. If you make him think less of himself and he feels he has no control over you, then you are free.

A lot has been said about narcissists and the red flags on a first date as to how they appear, what they say, and how to avoid the rest of the date. It's better to prevent getting into a relationship with a monster from the very first date.

One needs to pay rapt attention to locate these few signs adequately. Some narcissists don't know they are narcissists and if you tell them, they will not agree with you. Rule out every notion to save them because you may end up getting heartbroken. Protect yourself first.

Conclusion

The world of the narcissist is filled with chaos and pain. These things come from the damage they do to others as well as the harm they do to themselves through their dysfunctional behavior. As seen in true stories of narcissistic abuse, the narcissist abuses others to fill a need in themselves, but they also create circumstances that create chaos and pain around them.

The narcissist does not fully understand the pain they cause others because of the manner in which they perceive the world: as something to control to obtain what they need. The narcissist does not see others as feeling the way they feel because other people will never be important to them as they themselves are. They are a species apart, which allows them to abuse without remorse.

Healing from narcissistic abuse requires that you not only understand how the narcissist operates and but also the signs of the abuse in yourself. We began the process of healing from this form of abuse by learning more about narcissism.

There are certain traits that identify the narcissist. We all know that a narcissist is vain, but men and women with this condition are also remarkable for their grandiosity, sense of uniqueness, entitlement, need for admiration, lack of empathy, and delusional thinking. Narcissists are also experts at manipulation and prone to the emotional abuse of others.

You learned who the narcissist targets and why as a precursor to learning how to protect yourself. Narcissistic abuse often surfaces as emotional abuse, but there are other types. Abuse can lead to trauma, which can worsen illness or cause a new mental illness. Stopping abuse involves first recognizing that abuse is happening and then putting your guard up. You learned how being careful what you say to the narcissist and blocking their attempts to establish false rapport with you can be a very effective tool.

Once you have developed an idea of how to protect yourself, you are ready to devote time to healing. Healing from narcissistic abuse is not easy, in part because it can take the form of trauma, and such trauma can last a lifetime. Victims of narcissistic abuse can be similar to people with post-traumatic stress disorder, experiencing reliving events and hypervigilance long after the inciting factor has passed. Healing means devoting time to self-help and self-care. Medication and therapy are solid options but learning how to be confident and feel joy again is also important.

Healing for the narcissist often involves therapy, as with other personality disorders, and it is a very long process. Narcissism is not well-known because it isn't easy to deal with, but now you have the tools to help yourself and others survive the abuse that comes from being trapped in a particularly dangerous spiderweb.

www.ingramcontent.com/pod-product-compliance
Lightning Source LLC
Chambersburg PA
CBHW050030130526
44590CB00042B/2423